100 GREAT children's PICTURE BOOKS

LAURENCE KING

Published in 2015 by
Laurence King Publishing Ltd
361–373 City Road
London EC1V 1LR
Tel +44 20 7841 6900
Fax +44 20 7841 6910
www.laurenceking.com
enquiries@laurenceking.com

Cover, jacket and title page illustrations:
Sara Fanelli
Design: www.zoebather.co.uk
Photography: Ida Riveros (with the exception
of pages 16–21, 26–27, 36–37, 52–55)

A catalogue record of this book is available
from the British Library.

ISBN 978 1 78067 408 7

Printed in China

100 GREAT children's PicTuRe BoOKs

Martin Salisbury

Contents

Page from *Praia mar* by Bernardo Carvalho (see page 195).

Introduction

Having had the impertinence to make a selection under the banner of *100 Great Children's Picturebooks*, I am anxious to make a few things clear in my defence at the outset. First, I am of course very aware that, as a multi-modal form of communication, the successful picturebook is about much more than good art and design. This selection, however, is first and foremost about good art and design, and is made entirely on that basis. It aspires to deliver a visual feast for those who love the picturebook.

To borrow the title of Diana Klemin's 1966 book, the art of art for children's books has come increasingly under the spotlight. As various forms of screen media proliferate, the picturebook continues to thrive in printed form as an artefact to be shared and loved. More and more adults search second-hand bookshops and websites for first editions of picturebooks that they grew up with but have long since lost, to fulfil a need for the intimacy of physical contact with, and ownership of, something that played a crucial role in the development of a sense of self. Such is the power of the book.

I have shamelessly expanded the definition of 'children's picturebook' to include some books that may, in the view of many, not be deemed to have been designed strictly for children, alongside others that do not conform to the modern definition, based on an inseparable word–image union.

Today's thriving market in 'collectable' or 'vintage' children's books is accompanied by a growing interest in collecting original artworks from published children's books. Of course, with many of today's illustrators employing varying degrees of digital intervention in the creation of 'artwork', pre-digital originals are increasing in value. But it is the printed books themselves that I am concerned with here, and, having been given the impossibly difficult but hugely privileged task of selecting 100 titles from the last 100 or so years, I have opted for a luxuriously subjective approach. I have made my selection on rather un-academic, unscientific criteria, ultimately based on the 'wow factor'.

Many of these books are from my own 'collection'. I should point out that I am not a true collector; I do not tend to own or seek out pristine first editions, and many of the books photographed are visibly grubby and well used, as indeed they should be. Many have been begged and borrowed from friends, colleagues and students, both current and former. I am much indebted to all of them, and to friends from around the world who have introduced me to so many books from their cultures. Many of the books here have been photographed directly from their first editions. A few have come from important library collections, such as those at the University of Chicago and at Merano public library in northern Italy (the ÒPLA Collection).

To continue with my excuses, I have not attempted in any way to create a particularly even spread in terms of geography or time in this selection. There is an inevitable profusion of titles from 1950s and 1960s Britain, this bottleneck coming about partly because this was such an exciting time and place in the development of the children's picturebook, and partly because it was the time and place of my own childhood. There are also one or two artists who appear more than once in these pages. This is because they are of particular stature and importance, but in truth it is also a result of endless hours of trying to choose only one book from, in each case, such a rich corpus of work.

Looking at the visual cornucopia laid out in this book, it is reassuring to know that museums and libraries are at last beginning to recognize the importance of children's book illustration to our cultural heritage. The Japanese have led the way for some time, with such institutions as the Chihiro Art Museum and the Brian Wildsmith Museum of Art. There is also the wonderful Eric Carle Museum of Picture Book Art in the United States. Here in the UK we now have the National Centre for Children's Books at Seven Stories in Newcastle, which holds several key archives of artwork, books, manuscripts and correspondence between artists and publishers. We also have the House of Illustration in London, the realization of a long-standing dream of Sir Quentin Blake, who has done so much to promote the children's picturebook, both through his own illustrations and through his tireless public work.

In the course of my own work I encounter thousands and thousands of picturebooks, old and new, from all over the world. I have been fortunate enough to sit in judgement over them as a member of international awards juries at global book fairs. I have waded through the hundreds of publishers' stands at those same fairs. On a daily basis I look at the sketchbooks, notebooks and picturebooks-in-progress of master's students who are aspiring to a career in the field. Their passion for the subject is a continuing source of inspiration, and the thrill of seeing a beautiful picturebook emerge from a sketchbook never leaves me.

It is my hope that this book will appeal not only to illustration students and bibliophiles but also to anyone who enjoys beautiful things that can be owned, held and enjoyed over and over again.

Martin Salisbury

The physical shape of
the book forms the basis
of the running joke of
the runaway buggy as it
accelerates towards the
centre of the book.

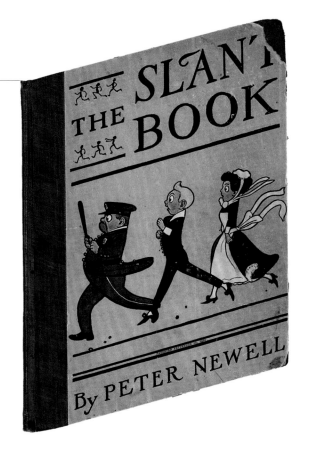

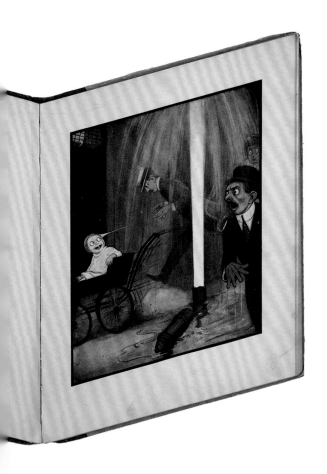

Then through a Watermelon patch
This awful cart descended,
And split the melons by the batch—
The Farmer was offended

And tried to stop its wild career,
Which was a silly notion—
It passed him promptly to the rear
With quite a rapid motion!

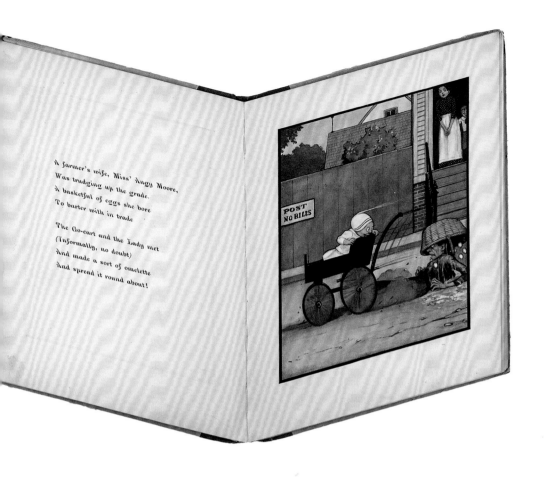

A farmer's wife, Miss' Angy Moore,
Was trudging up the grade.
A basketful of eggs she bore
To barter with in trade

The Go-cart and the Lady met
(Informally, no doubt)
And made a sort of omelette
And spread it round about!

Peter Newell
Published by Harper & Brothers,
New York, 1910
This copy: 1st edition
225 x 180 mm (9 x 7 in)

Twenty-first-century picturebooks are often preoccupied with postmodern parody and self-referentiality, as more and more books are created that feature interaction with their own physical format. It is easy to forget that Peter Newell was doing this sort of thing more than 100 years ago. *The Slant Book* is perhaps one of his most famous. It has been republished many times, and in many languages in recent years.

The book is rhomboid in shape, with text on the verso page and image on the recto throughout. The story follows the chaos of a runaway baby's buggy as it rolls down a hill, the gradient of which is exactly equal to the slope of the book, so that the delighted baby is seen to be rolling towards the gutter of the book on each double-page spread. Earlier books by Newell included *Topsys and Turvys* (1893), which could be read upside down or right side up, and *The Hole Book* (1908), which had a hole drilled through each page, following the path of a bullet.

Newell's books came late in his career, after many years of contributing humorous drawings to leading American periodicals, including *Scribner's Magazine* and the *Saturday Evening Post*. A collection of Newell's drawings and correspondence is held at Yale University's Beinecke Rare Book and Manuscript Library.

The illustrations are printed in two-colour half-tone, sometimes with less than perfect registration.

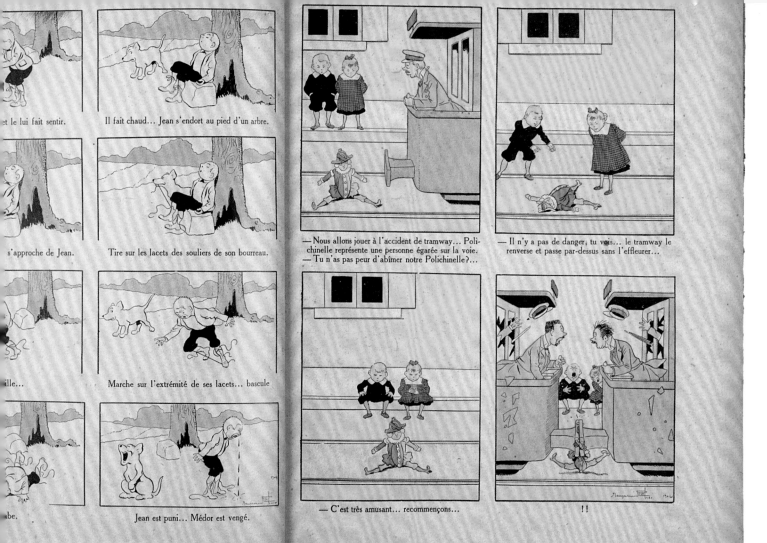

et le lui fait sentir. | Il fait chaud... Jean s'endort au pied d'un arbre.

s'approche de Jean. | Tire sur les lacets des souliers de son bourreau.

Marche sur l'extrémité de ses lacets... bascule

Jean est puni... Médor est vengé.

— Nous allons jouer à l'accident de tramway... Polichinelle représente une personne égarée sur la voie.
— Tu n'as pas peur d'abîmer notre Polichinelle?...

— Il n'y a pas de danger, tu vois... le tramway le renverse et passe par-dessus sans l'effleurer...

— C'est très amusant... recommençons...

!!

LE CHAPELET DE SAUCISSES OU LE VER GIGANTESQUE

LA TAUPE. — Quelle aubaine... voilà de quoi me nourrir pendant quelques semaines...

!!!

LE CANARD. — Quelle aubaine... voilà un ver de terre d'une jolie grosseur qui rentre dans son trou...

LE CANARD. — Je le tiens... il était temps...

LE CANARD. — Ce ver me paraît bien lourd...

LE CANARD. — C'est renversant! Inouï! Inimaginable!... Jamais je n'ai vu un ver de terre de cette longueur!

HISTOIRE DE MI-CARÊME

LE RENARD. — Oh! la belle poule!...

LE RENARD. — Elle est à moi!...

LE RENARD. — Pas encore!...

Rabier's experience as an animator is evident throughout these comic sequences, with figures frequently moving through static framing in short time frames.

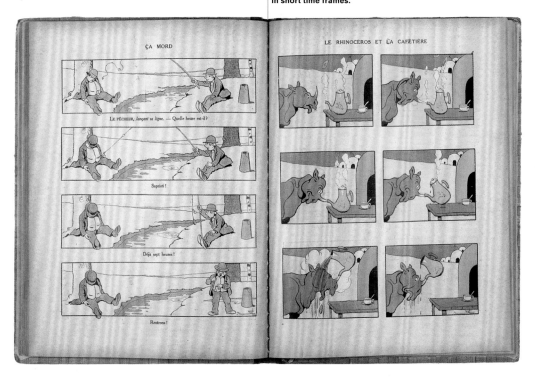

02
Le fond du sac
(The bottom of the bag)

Benjamin Rabier
Published by Librairie Garnier
Frères, Paris, 1912
This copy: 1st edition
305 x 230 mm (12 x 9 in)

Rabier is a key figure in the development of the picturebook. He was one of the first to give lead roles to animals as characters in comics, children's books and animated films; in the case of the films, he did so considerably in advance of the arrival of Disney. It is also generally accepted that Rabier's work had a major influence on Hergé's creation Tintin. In all, Rabier was responsible for around 250 illustrated books, most of them his own concepts.

Rabier was born in 1864 in the town of La Roche-sur-Yon in western France. Early works, such as *Tintin-Lutin* (1887, written in collaboration with Fred Isly), featured human characters, but Rabier was soon to become best known for the creation of two animal characters: the Laughing Cow (La vache qui rit), which advertises the cheese of the same name, and the storybook (and, later, cartoon) character Gédéon the duck.

Film-maker Mark Faye's animated documentary *Benjamin Rabier: The Man Who Made the Animals Laugh* (Novanima Productions, 2012) tells the story of Rabier's rise to fame from humble origins, working nights as an inspector at Paris's Les Halles markets. For many years he combined this mundane work with his developing career as an artist – a combination that perhaps drove him to take on too much illustration work and suffer a serious mental breakdown as a result.

Le fond du sac is a collection of 'shorts' – single-page comic sequences that feature both human and animal characters.

Son œuvre accomplie, Cavelier de la Salle, entouré de ses courageux compagnons, prend solennellement possession de la Louisiane.
Accourus de toutes parts, les chefs des nombreuses tribus indiennes viennent rendre hommage au grand Français et lui font leur soumission.

...gueurs d'un terrible hiver qui
...ux dans les glaces et les neiges.

...décidés à le suivre. On juge de
...illet de la même année, débarqua
...ût vus en France.

...rapports de son pilote, le Roi se
...olonisation. Il fallut l'intervention
...val, que Cartier avait gagné à sa

...ce-roi et de lieutenant-général des
.... mérité que lui.

...mirent à la voile le 23 Mai 1541,
...mplet, à la rivière de Sainte-Croix.
...aimait ses aises, trouva fort peu
...atin, il annonça qu'il allait chercher

...remier. Cartier attendit en vain les
...voyant pas revenir, il se décida à
...son tour à rentrer en France.

En cours de route, il
...rencontra les vaisseaux de M. le
...lieutenant-général qui, l'hiver
...passé, s'en revenait majestueuse-
...sement au Canada. De la Roque
...lui intima l'ordre d'avoir à re-
...brousser chemin. Mais Cartier,
...peu soucieux d'obéir à un
...homme qui commandait si bien
...et agissait si mal, continua sa
...route et débarqua à Saint-Malo.

Les Chefs Indiens concluent un pacte d'alliance avec Cartier. Pendant
la fête, les femmes de la tribu exécutent des danses dans l'eau.

Le roi Charles X récompensa, comme il le méritait, le courageux capitaine Dillon, q...
avait trouvé sur la fin de La Pérouse et de ses infortunés compagnons ces triste...
renseignements.

A l'île Vanikoro même, Dumont Durville dressa un monument. Aux antipodes de
France, dominant les flots mystérieux, il porte gravés pour l'éternité les noms de La Pérouse
et de ceux qui, avec lui, donnèrent noblement leur vie, pour la gloire de la France et
bien de l'Humanité.

La vie de La Pérouse est une remarquable leçon. Suivez-le, dès sa jeunesse ! Son pay...
est en proie aux attaques de ses ennemis. Dédaignant la vie plus facile, que lui permettrait so...
rang, il s'engage dans la marine, pour la défense de la France. Homme d'action, c'est dar...
l'action qu'il conquiert ses grades ; mais, dans le plus fort de la bataille, il sait se montrer, e...
même temps homme de bonté et de cœur : c'est ainsi que chargé de détruire des établissemen...
ennemis dans la baie d'Hudson, il accomplit strictement sa mission ; mais aussitôt après, i...
n'écoute que son cœur, et prend, en quelque sorte, sous sa protection, ceux que l'implacab...
loi de la guerre lui aurait permis de laisser périr.

Plus tard, nous le retrouvons à la tête de l'expédition en Océanie, qui a immortalisé so...
nom. Comme il l'a fait par les armes, il veut faire rayonner le nom de la France par le prestig...
plus durable de la science. La mission qu'on lui confie est difficile et périlleuse ; d'autre...
comme le célèbre navigateur anglais Cook, y ont laissé leur vie ; La Pérouse le sait ; néan...
moins il l'accepte avec joie. Au cours de ce voyage même, comme un avertissement du sort qu...
l'attend, il voit son fidèle ami, le capitaine de l'Angle, mourir sous les coups des sauvage...
Il continuera quand même. Ce que fut cette expédition, on le sait. Les renseignements précieu...
qu'il recueillit pour la science, les bénéfices qu'en tirèrent les navigateurs qui vinrent après lu...
nous les avons résumés.

Certes on peut déplorer sa mort et la perte des derniers documents qu'il avait recueilli...
et qui auraient augmenté le résultat matériel de son laborieux voyage. L'enseignement moral
qui s'en dégage n'en est pas moins grand. Les explorateurs, les grands chercheurs
qui vinrent après lui n'eurent qu'à suivre son exemple ; et maintenant
encore, ceux qui liront le drame poignant et magnifique que fut sa
vie, sentiront cet enthousiasme que donne le spectacle d'un
caractère vraiment fort et beau, mis au service
du bien commun.

03

Voyages et glorieuses découvertes des grandes navigateurs (The voyages and glorious discoveries of the great seafarers)

Edy Legrand
Published by Tolmer, Paris, 1921
This copy: 1st edition
390 x 280 mm (15¼ x 11 in)

One of the most important and influential book illustrators of the twentieth century, Edy Legrand has to be seen as something of an infant prodigy when one looks at his career as a whole. This magnificent book was produced two years after his better-known *Macao et Cosmage*, an astonishing debut at the age of 18. Both books feature stencilled 'pochoir' coloured line illustration.

The pochoir process (the use of metal stencils for hand-colouring with such water-based colour media as gouache or watercolour), with its Art Deco sensibility, was particularly popular in France for high-quality illustration after World War I – often under the supervision of Jean Saudé, a keen advocate of the technique. When used skilfully, as here, the results are spectacular, giving the colour a richness, depth and subtlety that is seldom seen with lithography. This is demonstrated to particular effect in a stunning double-page-spread illustration of Robert Cavelier and 'his courageous companions' receiving the homage of Native Americans as he takes possession of Louisiana.

Decorated letterforms open each chapter, and two fold-out illustrated maps further enhance the sumptuous production. The book is printed on heavyweight cartridge paper, and this copy shows evidence of excessive pressure used with the letterpress printing, which leaves its impression as the text forces its way through to be embossed into the reverse side of the images.

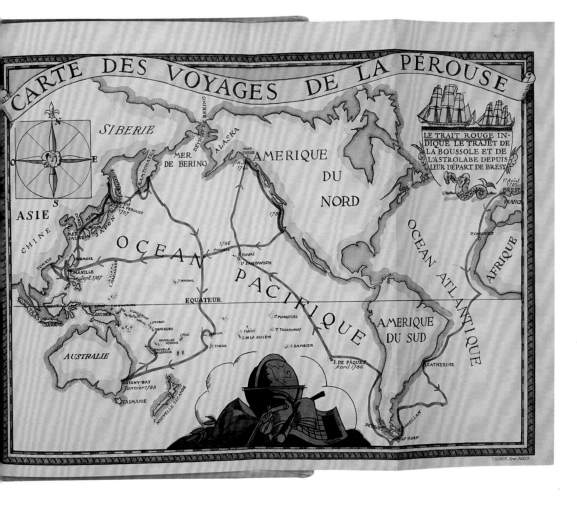

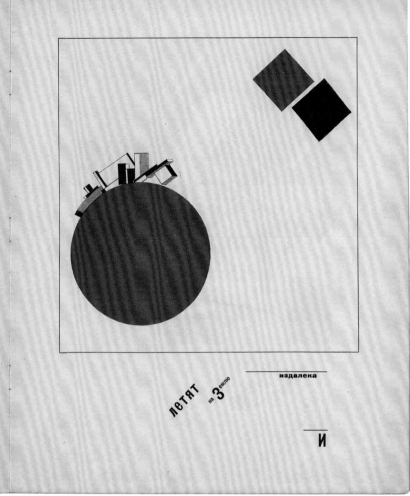

летят на 3 <del>версте</del>   издалена

И

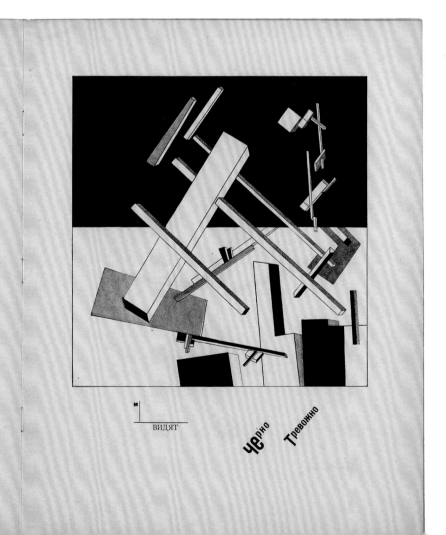

и

ВИДЯТ

черно Тревожно

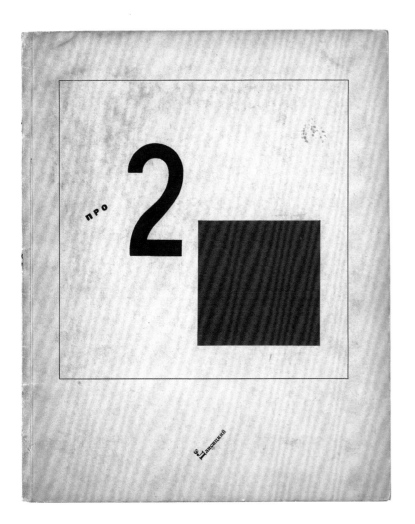

Printed in red and black with simple white stapled wrappers, *Pro dva kvadrata*'s geometrically expressed narrative embodies its author's aesthetic and political zeal.

04
Pro dva kvadrata (About two squares)

El Lissitzky
Published by Scythians,
Berlin, 1922
This copy: 1st edition
280 x 225 mm (11 x 9 in)

For a period of 20 or so years after the Russian Revolution of 1917, the harnessing of graphic art to the political objectives of the Soviet Union resulted in a period of highly inventive and influential work in children's books and poster design. The period has been re-evaluated in recent years and brought to wider attention through books and exhibitions, such as the 2011 exhibition and accompanying publication 'Adventures in the Soviet Imaginary', featuring the collection of the University of Chicago Library.

El Lissitzky was at the forefront of the Russian Suprematist movement. At the time of the publication of *Pro dva kvadrata* he was serving as the Russian cultural ambassador to Weimar Germany. He strongly propounded the view that artists should be agents of change, politically and culturally. His expression for this was *das zielbewußte Schaffen*, or 'goal-oriented creation'. This, his best-known book, certainly conforms to these ideals, expressing through Constructivist book design the triumph of the red square of modernity over the black square of conservative decadence. Regarded as one of the most seminal avant-garde artists' books of its time, in 2012 a first-edition copy sold at Christie's in London for £15,000 ($25,000).

From 1919, El Lissitzky taught at the People's Art School in Vitsyebsk, founded by fellow Jewish artist, Marc Chagall. He remained a champion of Constructivist art, whose mission he said was 'not to embellish life but to organize it'.

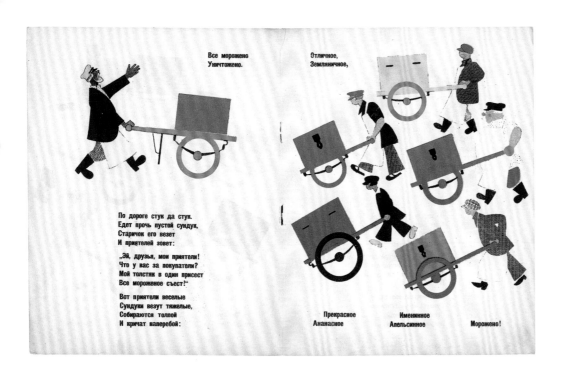

Все морожено
Уничтожено.

Отличное,
Земляничное,

По дороге стук да стук.
Едет прочь пустой сундук,
Старички его везет
И приятелей зовет:

„Эй, друзья, мои приятели!
Что у вас за покупатели?
Мой толстяк в один присест
Все мороженое съест!"

Вот приятели веселые
Сундуки везут тяжелые,
Собираются толпой
И кричат наперебой:

Прекрасное   Именинное
Ананасное   Апельсинное   Морожено!

С.МАРШАК
МОРОЖЕНОЕ
РИСУНКИ
В.ЛЕБЕДЕВА
РАДУГА
1925

Vladimir Lebedev's cover
design seamlessly fuses text
and image to form a graphic
representation of an ice-
cream vendor's cart.

На спине его сугроб,
Побелел блестящий лоб,
На очках узоры льдистые,
В серебре усы пушистые.

Ребятишки босиком
Ходят вслед за сундуком.
Остановится сундук,—
Все становятся вокруг.

Сахарно мороженно
На блюдечки положено,
Густо и сладко,
Ешь без остатка!

К сундуку бежит толстяк.
От жары он весь размяк,
Щеки, как подушки,
Шляпа на макушке.

„Эй,—кричит он,— старичок!
Положи на пятачок!"

Он стоит и не шевелится,
А кругом шумит метелица!

Lebedev worked in a
variety of idioms and was
constantly experimenting.
In *Morozhenoe* he uses
geometrical, mechanically
drawn shapes to create
highly stylized, Art Deco-
inspired figures.

Morozhenoe (Ice Cream)

Samuil Marshak, illustrated by
Vladimir Lebedev
Published by Raduga,
Leningrad, 1925
This copy: 1st edition
275 x 220 mm (10¾ x 8¾ in)

One of the most important
partnerships of the great days
of Soviet picturebooks was
that between the eminent writer
Marshak and the brilliantly
innovative painter and graphic
artist Lebedev. Together they
produced a number of striking
and highly influential children's
books that were much imitated
and brought style and colour to
the bookshops of the day.

Marshak achieved a high
level of prestige as a prolific writer
for the young, as well as being
a publisher, translator and critic.
He had studied in St Petersburg
and at the University of London.
After the Russian Revolution, he
became the head of the children's
department of Gosizdat, the state
publishing house in St Petersburg
(soon to be re-christened
Leningrad). After the dismantling
of the Stalinist publishing system
following Stalin's death in 1953,
Marshak went on to write for
children until his death in 1964.

Lebedev was born in St
Petersburg and studied at various
private studios there and at the
Academy of Fine Arts. He accepted
the post of art director of the
children's department alongside
Marshak at the Gosizdat, and
the close understanding between
the two led to a number of classics
of the period, including *Circus*,
Morozhenoe and *Book of Many
Colours*. Lebedev was closely
involved with a number of artists
working in children's books at that
time, including such key figures
as Kazimir Malevich and Vladimir
Mayakovsky. After receiving harsh
criticism of his work from some
quarters in the mid-1930s, Lebedev
began to work in a less avant-
garde, softer manner.

Bulanov's illustrations employ areas of delicate graphic mark making overlaid on flat colour, alongside formal Constructivist typography.

ПОТОП

СПОЛОЦКИЙ

РИСУНКИ
Д.БУЛАНОВА

РАДУГА

Вот плывет он меж домами,
Меж крутыми берегами.
Из окна течет река,
Удивляет моряка.
Залезает он в окошко,
На шкафу Мишук и кошка.
Мишуку: слезай-ка вниз!
А котенку: кис-кис-кис!
Не моргнул Мишук и глазом,
Соскочил с котенком разом.
С ними в кухне капитан
Под водою шарит кран.
Завернул его потуже:
— Будешь знать, как делать лужи!
И к окну шагает вброд
Капитан на пароход.

Только вот беда какая,
Без следа, без следа,
Удирает, утекая
Прочь, вода, вся вода.

Пароход рожден пловучим,
По воде ходить обучен.
Сел на землю, поднял вой:
— Не пойду по мостовой!

А народ бежит навстречу
И ведет такие речи:
— Ты, товарищ капитан,
Из чужих приехал стран.
Мы тебя встречаем славой,
Хоть сто лет морями плавай!

Вечер, ветер за окном,
Люди дома за столом.
И Мишук и прочие
Капитана подчуют.

А хвастливый самовар
Говорит, пуская пар:
— Я с водою не шучу,
Кипячу! Кипячу!

Кто герой? — Я герой!
У меня живот горой,
В нем горячая вода,
— Да!

Льет вода, земля дрожит,
Впереди народ бежит.
Через улицу и площадь
Мчат трамваи, скачет лошадь.

А вослед течет река
Глубока и широка,
И плывут вдоль реки
Караси и судаки.

А у нас-то во дворе
Сидит кот на фонаре.
Он мяучит, беспокоясь:
— Нужен пробковый мне пояс!

Но волна идет горою —
Тумака дает герою.
Ей плита кричит: — Не тронь, —
Обожжет тебя огонь! —
Но огонь дрожит и тухнет,
А вода течет по кухне;

Вот в окошко потекла
Из разбитого стекла.

На дворе сегодня праздник,
Детвора речонку дразнит:
— Речка к нам течет сюда,
В речке грязная вода.
Ты пришла, вода сырая,
Из подвала, из сарая? —
А вода бежит вперед,
Волны катит и ревет.
Детвора в испуге пятится,
Начинается сумятица.

Figures are static and posed,
giving the impression of flat,
cut-outs.

Semion Polotsky, illustrated by
Dmitri Bulanov
Published by Raduga,
Leningrad, 1925
This copy: 1st edition
215 x 190 mm (8½ x 7½ in)

Bulanov was a poster designer, painter and theatre designer who created a handful of picturebooks in the 1920s. He was born in 1898 in Nizhny Novgorod, the great-grandson of the Decembrist Vasily Ivashev, grandson of the feminist Maria Trubnikova and son of the revolutionaries Anatoly Bulanov and Olga Trubnikova. He died in a prison hospital at Zlatoust in 1942, having been arrested and sentenced to ten years in corrective labour camps.

Following the Russian Revolution Bulanov trained as a poster artist at the State Free Art Studios in St Petersburg (soon to be re-christened Leningrad) and by 1919 his work had been featured in an exhibition. In 1923 he became the chief designer on the magazine *Life of Art*, while also contributing design and illustration to a range of other publications. He would later work for the state advertising agency. His largest output was in the area of poster design. Much of this was in the arena of political propaganda, but he also created designs for posters and advertisements for Leningrad Zoo.

William Nicholson was
one of the first to create
interplay between words
and pictures, allowing
for interaction between
child, book and parent.

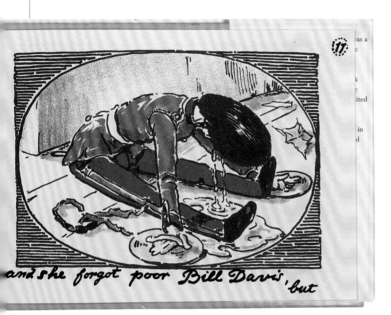

and she forgot poor Bill Davis, 'but

and he ran—

Mary replied

"O! I must take Apple Grey" said Mary
"and my gloves with the thumbs and

This landscape format was very rare at the time of publication.

07
Clever Bill

William Nicholson
Published by William Heinemann, London, 1926
This copy: 1999 facsimile edition (Heinemann)
170 x 235 mm (6¾ x 9¼ in)

Generally acknowledged as one of the key publications in the development of the picturebook as we know it today (along with Nicholson's *The Pirate Twins*, published by Faber in 1929), *Clever Bill* combined word and image in a way that we are now familiar with but which was daring for its time. The crudely handwritten verbal text acts mainly as a prompt to the reader to look more closely at the visual text in order to understand the narrative. In the words of American author and illustrator Maurice Sendak (see pages 89 and 145): 'Among the few perfect picturebooks ever created … I would not hesitate to give this to any child I knew.'

This is a simple story of a girl receiving a letter from her aunt, inviting her to come and stay. She tries to pack all of her toys into her suitcase but forgets the all-important Clever Bill, who has to make his own way in pursuit of the train until the two are reunited.

At the time of the creation of this book, Nicholson was nearing the end of his long career as a highly regarded painter and graphic artist, although he continued to exhibit until his death in 1949. He had also illustrated Margery Williams's iconic *The Velveteen Rabbit* in 1922.

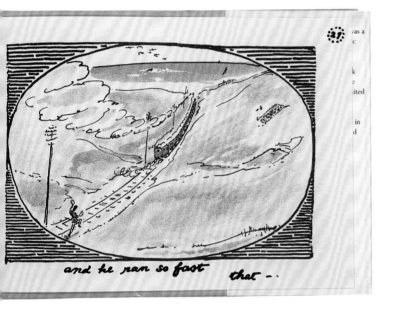

and he ran so fast that –

The crudely handwritten text is created in the same weight of line as that used in the image, and is used to increase the urge to turn the page.

first she packed it this way and

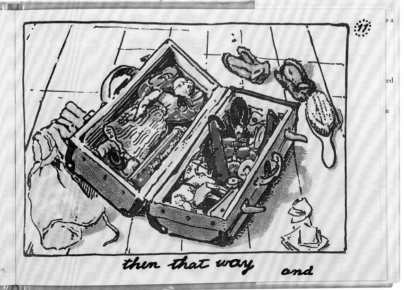

then that way and

There have been many editions of *Bonaventura*. This 1952 copy features a beautifully designed dust jacket over boards printed with a simple motif.

SCA CONGIURA

na nel baraccone. Cecè e Bonaventura Anche il cane fa per seguirli, ma Bar-e è tornato con un plico del tutto si-llo del milione e una grossa salciccia, con un fischio, agitando la salciccia per lla vista il cane si arresta e comincia a e. Barbariccia gli getta lontano la sal-ne si precipita ad addentarla e abban-one per terra. Immediatamente Barba-pprofitta per rubarlo, lasciando al suo o simile. Appena finita la sostituzione, a si riaffaccia alla porta del serraglio.

iato,
?

occupato a mangiare, gli strappa la sal-

ottone!

riuscendo appena a schivare una pe-adrone, scappa nel serraglio. Bonave-re lo segue, si accorge del plico abban-rra.

il milione!

e, lo spolvera ed entra nel baraccone. , rimasto solo col milione, gongola di gia.

ledetta...
Te l'ho fatta!...
a vendetta!...
schiatta... schiatta!...

lla, sventolando il milione come una quando un urlo improvviso all'interno io l'arresta di colpo con un piede per sto urlo l'orchestra attacca una musica are l'annunzio di un temporale vicino, negonda si precipita in scena strappan-ome.

UNA LOSCA CONGIURA

per chi mi rovescia i pupazzi
c'è un premio di tre caramelle!...
Correte, garzoni e donzelle!

CUNEGONDA
Venite venite, signori...
Spettacolo adatto a famiglie.
Venite... chi resta di fuori
non vede le mie meraviglie...
Venite venite, signori!

SCENA SECONDA
Il bellissimo Cecè e detti

Cecè è entrato durante le battute precedenti, guardandosi intorno con l'aria di chi cerca qualche cosa. Egli è sempre così in ammirazione della sua bellezza che le grida dei due lo lasciano estraneo.

CUNEGONDA
Venite venite a vedere
quest'oggi importanti debutti...

CECÈ
rivolgendosi alla padrona del serraglio; pieno di compitezza.
Mi scusi, vorrei per piacere...

CUNEGONDA
Con l'aria di chi tiene indietro una folla.
Adagio, c'è posto per tutti!
Cecè, un po' deluso, si rivolge all'altro.

BARBARICCIA
Grande è il divertimento

16

Tofano cleverly creates three colours out of two by using the white of the page to define the clothing of the figures.

NA LOSCA CONGIURA

...ia salire, Eccellenza:
...mo una cordiale accoglienza!

...comando alla vostra diligenza!
Via dal fondo.

SCENA QUARTA
ILARIA, poi CLEMENTE e ARIANNA

Appena uscito Cecè, Macario e Ilaria si dànno un gran da fare per mobilitare tutto il personale.

...te Valente Innocente Defendente!

...a Marianna Susanna Giovanna!

...e presto!
Entra Arianna di corsa; ha tutto un occhio ammaccato.

...quell'occhio pesto?

...ccidente di Felicetta
...rato nell'occhio la saponetta!
Entra Clemente: ha una fasciatura, come una farfalla, intorno alla punta del naso.

08
Il teatro di Bonaventura: una losca congiura (The theatre of Bonaventura: a shady conspiracy)

Sergio Tofano
Published by Edizioni Alpes,
Italy, 1930
This copy: Edizioni Rizzoli,
Italy, 1952
213 x 153 mm (8½ x 6 in)

Tofano was a multi-talented writer, actor, comedian, interpreter, designer and cartoonist whose graduation thesis at the University of Rome was rejected twice for its excessive use of humour. The character of Signor Bonaventura was originally created in 1917 and appeared first in the Sunday *Giournalino della Domenica*, then in the children's supplement, *Corriere dei Piccoli*. Scripted and drawn by Tofano, or 'STO' ('I AM') as he signed himself, the strip was in the form of a full page in eight vignettes with text in verse. It ran continuously for forty years and eventually moved from the page to the stage, where Tofano took on the role of his character. Bonaventura also graduated to the screen in 1945 in the form of the film *Cinderella and Signor Bonaventura*.

In 1923, Tofano married the actress and costume designer Rosetta Cavallari, who became his lifelong companion. As a designer, Tofano extended his influence beyond Italy, working for newspapers and magazines around the world, including as a long-standing contributor to *Vanity Fair* in Boston in the 1920s. In later years, much of Tofano's work centred on the theatre and the teaching of acting. His *Signor Bonaventura* series became so popular and so ubiquitous in the public consciousness of the time that it has been seen by some as the last 'mask' of the *commedia dell'arte*.

ы.

ех.

Там —

дым,

здесь —

гром.

Гро-

мим

весь

дом.

И вот

вылазит паровоз

чтоб вас

и нас

и нес

НА ЗАВОДЕ ХОРОШО

а, доктору —
лучше:
я б детей лечить пошел-
пусть меня научат.

Детям
я
лечу болезни—
где занятие полезней?
Я приеду к Пете,
я приеду к Поле.
—Здравствуйте, дети!
Кто у вас болен?
Как живете?
Как животик?

— Поставьте этот градусник
подмышку, детишки!—
И ставят дети радостно
градусник подмышки.
— Вам бы
очень хорошо
проглотить порошок
и микстуру
ложечкой
пить понемножечку.
Вам
в постельку лечь
поспать бы,
вам —
компресс на живот,
и тогда
у вас
до свадьбы
все конечно заживет.

ДОКТОРАМ ХОРОШО,

Boldly expressive letterforms insistently ask the question 'Whom shall I become' on Shifrin's dramatic cover design.

Vladimir Mayakovsky, illustrated by Nisson Abramovich Shifrin
Published by Molodaia Gvardiia, Moscow, 1931
This copy: 2nd edition
220 x 200 mm (8¾ x 7¾ in)

Poet and trained artist, Futurist theorist and passionate revolutionary, Mayakovsky placed his talents firmly at the service of political power. A close collaborator of Vladimir Lebedev (see page 19), another key figure in Soviet children's books, Mayakovsky wrote 14 poems for children, employing playful word associations that could be deconstructed and reassembled by their young readers.

In the catalogue accompanying the 2011 Chicago University exhibition 'Adventures in the Soviet Imaginary', Robert Bird suggests: 'Soviet children's books and posters owe a great deal of their inimical look and sound to the poet Vladimir Mayakovsky (1893–1930). Mayakovsky was the most prominent of many avant-garde artists who, driven by ideological commitment and financial exigency, transformed the popular media landscape of Russia over the course of the 1920s.'

Nisson Shifrin was born in 1892 in Moscow. After studying painting in Kiev, he worked mainly in theatre design; from 1935 to 1961 he was the principal stage designer at the Central Theatre of the Soviet Army. He also taught at several Moscow art schools.

Kem byt'? invited its readers to think about which important role they might take as a grown-up worker in Revolutionary Russia. Shifrin's designs echo and accommodate the non-linear nature of the text.

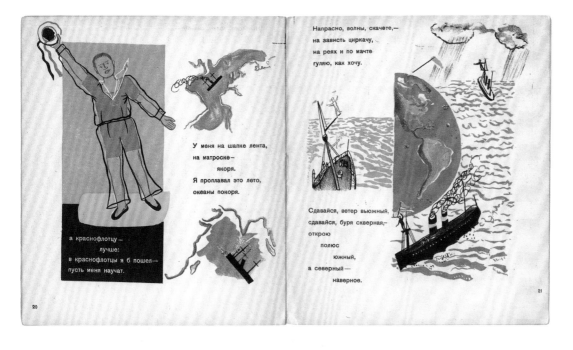

cher, who had a little stand on one side of Hansi's mother, hung up ...ality ducks and on the other side Frau Wunder stopped sprinkling ...es. They both looked at Hansi and made believe they did not know ...mountaineer. "Why, it's Hansi! Look at his brown knees and the ...is hat."

"Oh my, Frau Hofer, the taxes are getting worse every day. Where is one to get the money to pay for them, with times the way they have been this winter!"

"Don't talk, Frau Wunder," said Herr Fischer, holding up three fingers of his right hand. "Look at me—three ducks last week—that's all I sold. Read and write —three ducks—why, if I wasn't——"

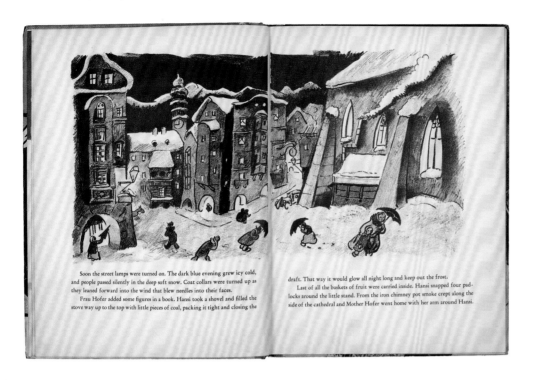

Soon the street lamps were turned on. The dark blue evening grew icy cold, and people passed silently in the deep soft snow. Coat collars were turned up as they leaned forward into the wind that blew needles into their faces.

Frau Hofer added some figures in a book. Hansi took a shovel and filled the stove way up to the top with little pieces of coal, packing it tight and closing the

draft. That way it would glow all night long and keep out the frost.

Last of all the baskets of fruit were carried inside. Hansi snapped four padlocks around the little stand. From the iron chimney pot smoke crept along the side of the cathedral and Mother Hofer went home with her arm around Hansi.

Bemelmans used lithographic crayon to draw each colour separation directly onto the plate, using the white of the page to suggest the continuing snowy foreground.

Ludwig Bemelmans
Published by the Viking Press,
New York, 1934
This copy: 1st edition,
2nd printing, 1937
310 x 235 mm (12¼ x 9¼ in)

Although best known for his subsequent, hugely popular Madeline books, Bemelmans' first picturebook was this semi-autobiographical tale of a childhood holiday in the Austrian Tyrol. Hansi is packed by his mother on to a little train, and journeys up into the mountains, where he stays with Uncle Herman, Aunt Amelie and their daughter, cousin Lieserl, for the Christmas holidays. Various adventures are described through words and pictures in a generously sized format, with alternating colour and black-and-white pages.

Born in 1898, the author had experienced a troubled upbringing in what was then Austrian territory (now Italian), and was sent to the United States at the age of 18 to work in the hotel industry, eventually opening his own restaurant. This first venture into writing and illustrating came at the suggestion of friends and was well received by reviewers. It marked the beginning of a successful career as a humorist, novelist and artist. Bemelmans' work was characterized by an idiosyncratic, occasionally sentimental approach to the anecdotal.

There is far more text here than would be found in a modern picturebook. It falls somewhere between an illustrated book and what we now think of as a picturebook, with several beautiful double-page-spread illustrations in colour. The printing was clearly produced auto-lithographically, and Bemelmans would have needed to produce separations for each colour directly on the plate; in places, he has overlaid colours to create further hues, thereby maximizing the potential of the process. He appears to have used both lithographic crayon and inks. Bemelmens' extremely limited – at times appalling – draughtsmanship is somehow always surmounted by the exuberance and charm of his vision.

Tim got more and more excited as
had never been

they neared the steamer as he
in one before.

Dramatic double-page
spreads are interspersed
with others showing
multiple images to speed
up the narrative.

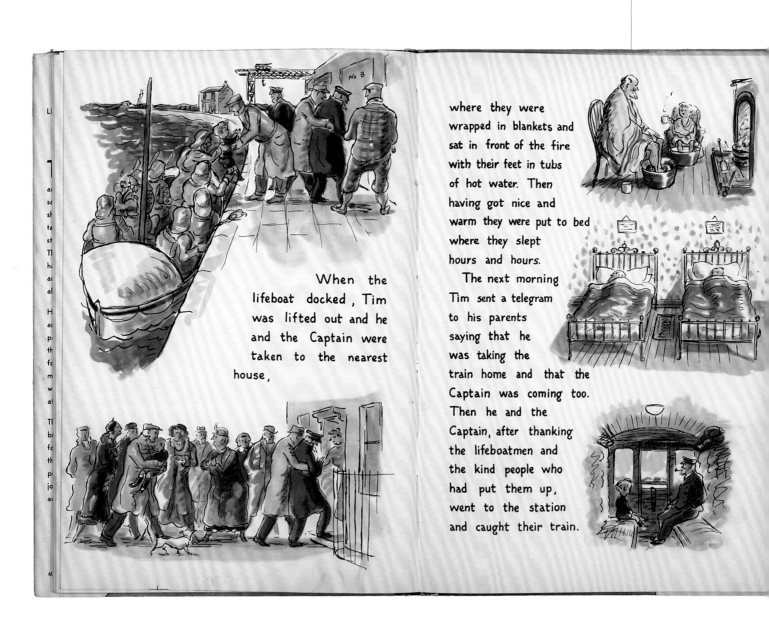

When the
lifeboat docked, Tim
was lifted out and he
and the Captain were
taken to the nearest
house,

where they were
wrapped in blankets and
sat in front of the fire
with their feet in tubs
of hot water. Then
having got nice and
warm they were put to bed
where they slept
hours and hours.
   The next morning
Tim sent a telegram
to his parents
saying that he
was taking the
train home and that the
Captain was coming too.
Then he and the
Captain, after thanking
the lifeboatmen and
the kind people who
had put them up,
went to the station
and caught their train.

The lifeboat came alongside and a life line was thrown to them, down which, first Tim, and then the Captain were drawn to safety. Hardly had they left the steamer when it sank beneath the waves.

Edward Ardizzone
Published by Oxford University
Press, Oxford, 1936
This copy: 1st edition
335 x 235 mm (13¼ x 9¼ in)

Ardizzone's first major work for children is something of a milestone in the history of the picturebook. As with the other books in the series, Ardizzone creates a world in which children casually head off to adventure at sea with parents nowhere to be seen. Much has been written about Ardizzone's work, with particularly valuable material from children's book critic Brian Alderson.

The first three Tim and Lucy books were produced in this large format, printed on one side of the paper only. Alderson speculates that this may have been due to the particularly humid summers in New York, where the book was printed, causing problems with the drying time for printing inks – or possibly for the simple reason that the large books felt too thin when the pages were printed on both sides, which may have led to some feeling that they were not getting their money's worth.[1] Ardizzone was familiar with Jean de Brunhoff's similarly sized Babar books, which had arrived successfully from France, and had apparently had his manuscript turned down by numerous publishers, perhaps because of its size.

Later Tim books were smaller in format, and Ardizzone developed a technique of drawing the black-ink line work on a separate transparent overlay so that it could be printed in a pure, solid black, rather than that composed of the four constituent print colours.

Ardizzone's iconic cover design feels extremely 'handmade', the roughness of the brushstrokes adding to the windswept feel.

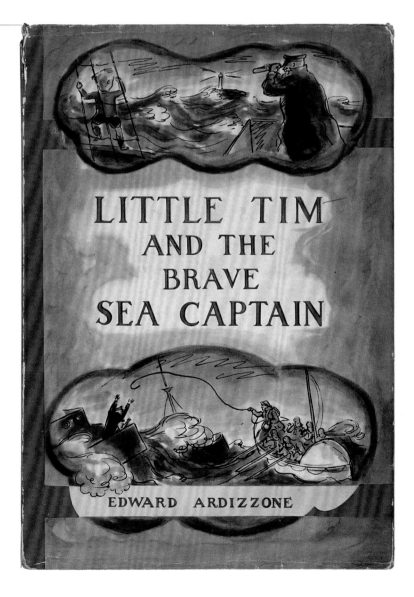

LITTLE TIM
AND THE
BRAVE
SEA CAPTAIN

EDWARD ARDIZZONE

1 'The Publishing of the Manuscript', by Brian Alderson, in *Edward Ardizzone: Little Tim and the Brave Sea Captain*, a facsimile of the original manuscript of the first edition of 1936 (Koguma Publishing, Tokyo, 2011).

Soon the great day for going into the country arrived. Mr. Grimes had bought a large car and all the luggage was piled on top of it. Lucy Brown was very excited.

Then had a le Smawley, that M very ill, to come She at her hat and coat over to Mr. Grimes' sat with him a lon

Ardizzone's text seems unthinkable in today's politically correct times.

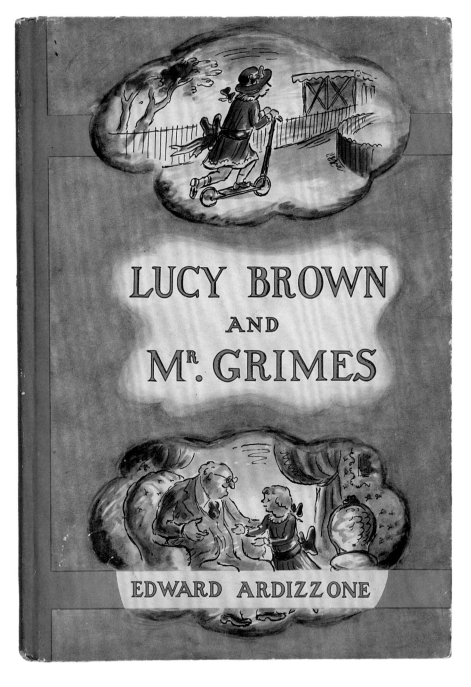

LUCY BROWN AND MR. GRIMES

EDWARD ARDIZZONE

The font, designed to give a handwritten effect, sits perfectly with the artist's relaxed and expressive line.

day she
rom Mrs.
ng her
es was
sking her
see him.
put on
hurried
ere she
, which

cheered him up a lot.
    Her visit seemed to do
him a little good, so she came
to see him every day for a
long time.
    Every day Mr. Grimes got
a little better, until one day
he was well enough to get up
in his dressing gown.

Every fine day   she went for a ride

12
**Lucy Brown and
Mr. Grimes**

Edward Ardizzone
Published by Oxford University
Press, Oxford, 1937
This copy: 1st edition
335 x 235 mm (13¼ x 9¼ in)

After being out of print for many
years, later editions of this book
were published with an altered
text as, even in the mid-twentieth
century, this tale of friendship
between a young girl and a lonely
old man was deemed worrisome
and inappropriate. This was
the second of Ardizzone's three
large-scale picturebooks of the
1930s (the final one was *Tim
and Lucy Go to Sea*, which was
published the following year),
and the book's text does seem
extraordinarily naive, even for
times that were less obsessed
with political correctness.

    This is our first introduction to
little Lucy, who lives with her aunt
and in later books goes on to have
many adventures with Tim – who
featured in Ardizzone's book of the
year before (see page 31). But here
she is befriended by the elderly
Mr Grimes, who announces: 'You
do look nice.' 'Thank you, sir,' says
Lucy Brown, 'I am very well and
would like a nice ice cream.' Mr
Grimes later becomes very ill, and,
after much attention from eminent
physicians, it is only a visit from
Lucy that brings him back to good
health. Mr Grimes then decides to
leave all of his money to little Lucy
and take her off to live with him in
the country!

    The colours of Ardizzone's
magnificent illustrations are
beautifully printed by W. S. Cowell
of Ipswich.

Ruled lines and rigid
perspective create highly
static, decorative designs.

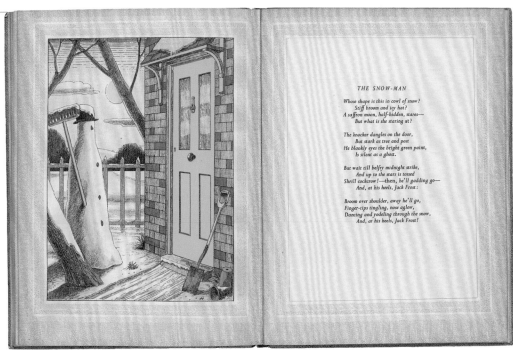

THE SNOW-MAN

Whose shape is this in cowl of snow?
  Stiff broom and icy hat?
A saffron moon, half-hidden, stares—
  But what is she staring at?

The knocker dangles on the door,
  But stark as tree and post
He blankly eyes the bright green paint,
  Is silent as a ghost.

But wait till belfry midnight strike,
  And up to the stars is tossed
Shrill cockcrow!—then, he'll gadding go—
  And, at his heels, Jack Frost:

Broom over shoulder, away he'll go,
  Finger-tips tingling, nose aglow,
Dancing and yodeling through the snow,
  And, at his heels, Jack Frost!

se,

ows
down—
town;

way:
?

hter:
after,

ter

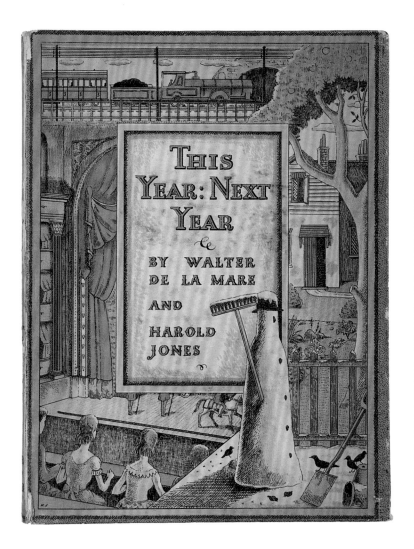

Each spread displays
an acute sense of design,
structure and pattern,
rather than a representation
of spatial depth.

13
This Year: Next Year

Walter de la Mare, illustrated by
Harold Jones
Published by Faber & Faber,
London, 1937
This copy: 1st edition
253 x 195 mm (10 x 7¾ in)

The poems of Walter de la Mare
have been illustrated by many
artists, notably Edward Ardizzone,
Claud Lovat Fraser and W. Heath
Robinson. Harold Jones made his
name with this, his first book, which
immediately announced him as a
highly individual new talent. It was
one of his finest achievements,
despite the many excellent books
that followed in a long career.

Jones's lithographs were printed
at the Baynard Press, one of a
handful of high-quality printers in
Britain in the mid-twentieth century.
The book was also carefully
designed throughout by Jones, with
each page framed by an individually
coloured border. A simple grid
format gives us an image, a block
of text or a combination of the two
in each of these frames. The artist's
meticulously decorative line work
is supported by flat colour in an
entirely static, carefully composed
manner, using ruled lines for the
representation of all man-made
shapes. There is a complete absence
of fluency or gestural mark making
in Jones's draughtsmanship, but a
magical sense of calm and reflection
that lends itself well to poetry.

Jones studied at Goldsmiths
and the Royal College of Art in
London, and later taught drawing
at the Ruskin School of Drawing
and Fine Art in Oxford. As well as
an illustrator, he was also a painter
and printmaker. His influence on
illustrators of more recent times has
been considerable and is openly
acknowledged by many, Ian Beck
being an example. Jones died in his
late eighties in 1992.

MODEL SHIPS AND R

All the models that this shop sells are sca
they are exact miniatures of the origina
reduced in the same proportion. And the
grown-up people as well as for children t
of people are interested, for example, in
work, and have complete miniature rai
out in a spare room or round their back
tunnels and embankments, sidings and go
stations; also a proper working signalling

Bassett-Lowke, which is the name of th
models in eight different sizes, the smalle
electricity on the dining-room table, hav
the track—the distance apart of the rail
about one-ninetieth full size. The usual
systems are 1¼ in. gauge and 1¾ in. gauge.
one forty-fifth and one thirty-second full
have clockwork or electric locomotives.
for outdoor railway systems, with real st
range from 2½ in. gauge up to 15 in., whi
quarter full size. These largest ones are po
haul train loads of real people. The engine
or more, they can travel at 35 miles an h
a load of 20 tons behind them. Basset-L
these to order, but their catalogue of loc
includes a 7¼ in. gauge (one-eighth full si
model of the L.M.S. express locomotive '
ing £500, and a 9½ in. gauge (one-sixth fu
'Atlantic' type locomotive and tender, cos
with mechanical lubricator and vacuum b

As realism in every detail is what mod
80

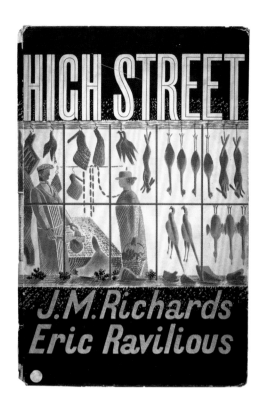

J. M. Richards, illustrated by
Eric Ravilious
Published by Country Life,
London, 1938
This copy: 1st edition
235 x 153 mm (9¼ x 6 in)

One of the iconic illustrated
books of the twentieth century,
High Street gives us a glimpse
of the interiors and exteriors
of British high-street shops in
the years leading up to World
War II. Ravilious had studied at
Eastbourne School of Art on the
south coast of England before
going on to London's Royal College
of Art in the early 1920s. There he
joined the famously talented group
of students who were to come
under the influence of tutor Paul
Nash in the design department.
These included Edward Bawden,
who was to become a close friend,
and Enid Marx, both of whom
appear elsewhere in this book
(see pages 51 and 109). The year
group as a whole was described
by Nash as an 'outbreak of talent'.
In recent years there has been a
surge of interest in the output of
these artists and others of the mid-
twentieth century who successfully
straddled the fine and applied arts.

The idea for *High Street* had
originated in discussions between
Ravilious and a fellow student,
Helen Binyon. They had planned it
as an 'Alphabet of Shops'. Ravilious
had recently learnt lithography, a
medium that he would go on to use
to great effect until his early death
while serving as an official war
artist in 1942.

The 24 shops depicted by
Ravilious in all their eccentricity
were real establishments. The
images combine beautifully with
the text by architectural historian
J. M. Richards, both being rather
droll in tone. Original copies
of the book are now scarce,
highly collectable and extremely
expensive to buy, many having
been broken up in order to sell
the illustrations individually.

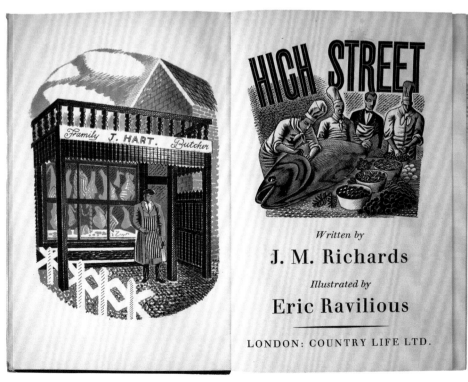

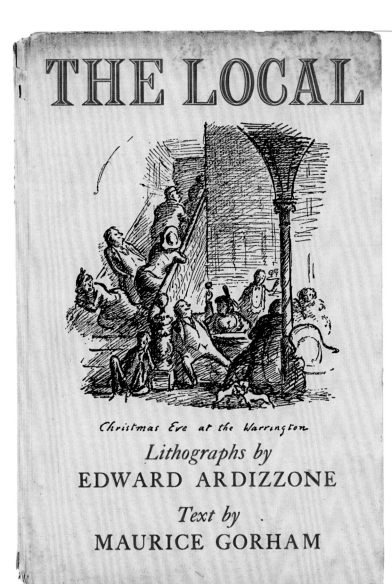

THE LOCAL

Christmas Eve at the Warrington

Lithographs by
EDWARD ARDIZZONE

Text by
MAURICE GORHAM

Despite a lack of any transparent overprinting to create further colours, Ardizzone's use of a range of tones in the black plate gives a strong sense of light.

Dining R

Lounge at the Warrington

... at the Spread Eagle

15
The Local

Maurice Gorham, illustrated by
Edward Ardizzone
Published by Cassell & Co.,
London, 1939
This copy: 1st edition
235 x 160 mm (9¼ x 6¼ in)

Along with Ravilious's *High Street*, published the previous year (see page 37), this is one of the key British illustrated books of the twentieth century. With his friend writer and broadcaster Maurice Gorham, Ardizzone lovingly explores one of his favourite subjects – the English pub. The book exudes in words and pictures the passion that both men feel for their subject.

Ardizzone's attention is as much on those who populate the featured establishments as on the buildings themselves. Each chapter loosely explores an aspect of pub culture, and is illustrated by a three- or sometimes four-colour lithograph, drawn by the artist directly on the plate. The prints are laden with narrative, anecdotal detail, informed by the hours that Ardizzone liked to spend in his favourite pubs in London's Maida Vale. He had clearly not mastered the technicalities of lithography – there is little or no use of overprinting to make extra colours – but the black lithographic crayon underpins and holds together the other colours, and is used superbly to suggest the smoky world of the pre-war pub.

The scarcity of this book today is due to the fact that most copies went up in flames when the warehouse in which they were being stored was bombed in the Blitz. After the war, the publisher Percival Marshall put out an edition with black-and-white line-drawn versions of the illustrations, with the title *Back to the Local*.

not a kids book!

LE PLUS BEAU PAYS DU MONDE

Le plus beau pays du monde
C'est la terre où je naquis ;
Au printemps, la rose abonde
Aux abords de ses courtils.
On y parle un doux langage,
Le plus beau qu'on ait formé ;
L'étranger devient plus sage,
Quand il se met à l'aimer.

Heureux qui reçut la chance
De l'ouïr dès le berceau ;
Car la langue de la France
Est un chant toujours nouveau.

Parfums de fleurs, chants de cloches,
Bruits d'eaux vives, gais frissons
Des tiges qui se rapprochent
Quand mûrissent les moissons ;
Etoiles dans un ciel tendre,
Sourires d'aube, en éveil ;
Ah ! mon pays, j'aime entendre
Ta chanson dans le soleil.

Philéas Lebesgue

90

LA COLOMBE

Messagère de l'avril,
Colombe, colombe,
Les hommes sont en péril,
Apporte la paix au monde
Colombe...

Toi qui reviens dans les branches,
Par delà le noir hiver,
Chante-nous pour les dimanches
Les grâces du rameau vert.

Messagère de l'avril,
Colombe, colombe,
Les hommes sont en péril,
Apporte la paix au monde
Colombe.

Francis Yard

91

AUTOMNE

Les feuilles tombent peu à peu,
Les feuilles sont déjà par terre,
En grand silence, en grand mystère,
Les feuilles tombent peu à peu.

Les pommes tombent sur les feuilles
Et brillent comme des joyaux,
Par les crépuscules royaux,
Les pommes tombent sur les feuilles.

Lucie Delarue-Mardrus

10

SIMONE, ALLONS AU VERGER

Simone, allons au verger
Avec un panier d'osier.
Nous dirons à nos pommiers,
En entrant dans le verger :
Voici la saison des pommes.
Allons au verger, Simone,
Allons au verger.

Remy de Gourmont

11

Selected by Marcelle Drouin,
illustrated by Michel Bouchaud
Published by Librairie Istra,
Paris/Strasbourg, 1939
This copy: undated,
probably reprint
225 x 180 mm (9 x 7 in)

Michel Bouchard was born into
an artistic family in Nantes in 1902
and, after studying at the Académie
Julian in Paris, he regularly exhibited
paintings and prints along with his
three brothers. He is best known,
however, for his work in advertising
and design in the 1920s and
1930s. He was part of a creative
team under the direction of Alfred
Tolmer for three years – a group
of talents from around Europe that
included Raymond Peynet.

Bouchard later worked for the
fashion magazines *Monsieur* and
Vogue, and designed many posters.
His elegant graphic work, evoking
the style and sophistication of
Parisian life at that time, became
synonymous with the promotion
and sale of luxury goods and travel.
He was also a successful designer
of logos and brand identities
before such terms were in general
use; in 1939 his emblem design
for a company formed from the
amalgamation of five publishing
houses came into use and is
still carried on some publications.

In that same year, *Mes belles
poésies* brought together a
collection of poetry aimed at French
primary-school children. The free-
standing illustrations suggest the
effects of stencilling and pochoir
techniques (see page 15). Soft,
flowing, rounded shapes echo the
rhythm and flow of the texts.

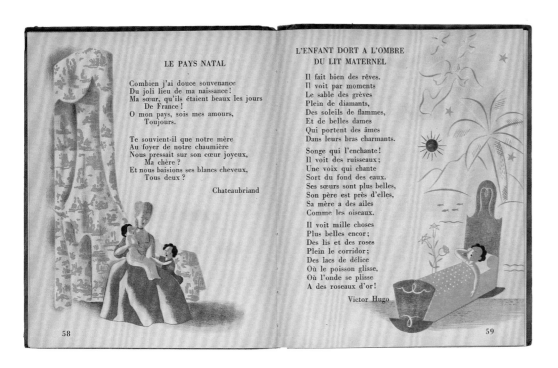

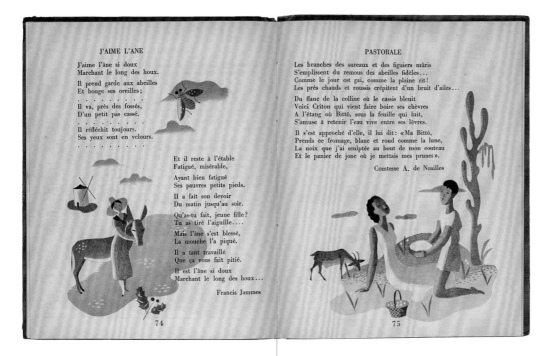

Throughout the book, the
illustrations are loose edged,
gently curling around the
text to provide a quiet visual
counterpoint.

He planted himself in the center of the road, raised one hand to stop the traffic, and then beckoned with the other, the way policemen do, for Mrs. Mallard to cross over.

She taught them how to swim an

They looked in Louisburg Square, but there was no water to swim in.

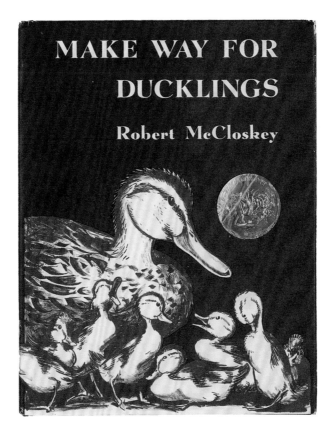

17
Make Way for Ducklings

Robert McCloskey
Published by the Viking Press,
New York, 1941
This copy: 1977 reprint
310 x 240 mm (12¼ x 9½ in)

Awarded the Caldecott Medal the year after its publication, this book has become one of the most enduring and iconic of American picturebooks. It had sold more than 2 million copies by 2003, the year of McCloskey's death. The book tells the story of a pair of mallard ducks in the city of Boston that are looking for a suitable place to raise a family. Its charm perhaps lies in the concerned efforts of policeman Michael, who leaps into action to hold up the traffic to allow the ducks and their eight chicks to cross the road. At 72 pages, the book is extremely long for a picturebook. Each spread contains a single, double-page image with text, the images having been drawn in charcoal and lithographed in sepia.

McCloskey's book was inspired by time spent feeding the ducks in the public gardens while studying at Boston's Vesper George School of Art in the 1930s. Later, when researching the book while in New York, it is said that he brought six ducklings home to his apartment to draw from observation. Certainly, there is a sense of the ducks being drawn with greater realism than the more stylized human figures. Critics of children's literature have produced all manner of theories and critiques on the book's gender stereotyping and plot shortcomings, but McCloskey always made it clear that he saw himself as an artist who happened to make children's books.

Here you can see a typical limestone Church Tower and the fine gables and chimneys of 17th century houses.
Two older houses can be seen at the bottom of the street, while the big building on the right is a tithe barn.

20

A TIMBER, PLASTER AND THATCH VILLAGE

The close and the more decorative timbering of the 15th century can be compared with the more open work of later years. The church spire is covered with wooden 'shingles'. Decorated thatching and plaster work can be seen. There is also a flint wall with brick edging, while the thatched wall is made of earth coated with plaster.

A BRICK AND TILE VILLAGE

This shows a 16th century timber framing filled with brick 'nogging'; a tile-hung house; weather boarding; and the simplicity of an 18th century 'stucco' covered house. At the top of the street is a low-fronted shop of the same period, and beyond a 17th century house in the new style.

44

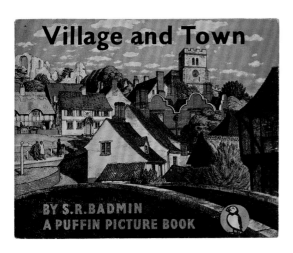

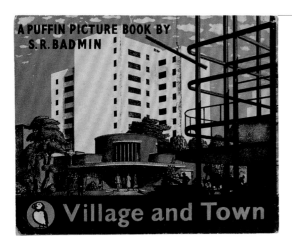

In creating the colour separations directly on the lithographic plate, Badmin would not see the full-colour outcome until it was printed. This demanded an unusual ability to separate and reassemble mentally the four constituent printing colours.

S. R. Badmin
Published by Puffin Picture Books, London, 1942
This copy: 1st edition
82 x 225 mm (3¼ x 9 in)

The Puffin Picture Books were the brainchild of Noel Carrington, who was well known in London publishing circles, and was the brother of the artist Dora Carrington. While working at Country Life (see *High Street* by J. M. Richards and Eric Ravilious, page 37) Carrington had become aware of publishers in France and Russia using auto-lithographic methods to create highly successful colour children's books at low cost, and wanted to develop something similar in the UK. He discussed this with Allen Lane, the man behind the iconic Penguin paperbacks, probably at the Double Crown Club. Lane was taken with the idea, and the project quickly took off. The key to this success was first of all the printing of each book on one very large sheet of paper (colour spreads on one side, and black-and-whites on the other) and, secondly, employing the artists to work directly on the lithographic plates themselves.

S. R. (Stanley Roy) Badmin's work for the series extended to three books. These are among the most affectionately remembered of the series for many who grew up with them. Badmin was a master of the English landscape, with a particular sensitivity to trees. His watercolours and etchings were familiar to collectors and the wider public alike, the latter through his many travel posters and book illustrations. Badmin's auto-lithographic separations for the Puffin Picture Books demonstrate his intense understanding of colour. The printed outcomes are seamless in their use of overlaid constituent parts.

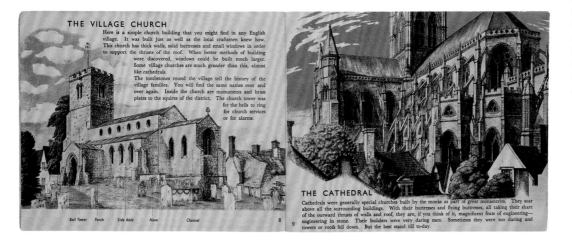

Malíř

Vezmi žlutou tužku,
namaluj mi hrušku
a pod hrušku talíř.
Sláva, ty jsi malíř!

A child's drawings are cleverly absorbed into the design of this spread, their colours having been carefully coordinated with the main image.

Blocks of colour and texture with no outlines give a pleasing 'printmaking' quality to Trnka's illustrations.

Počitadlo

Jedna, dvě,
Honza jde,

jedna, dvě, tři,
pes ho větří,

jedna, dvě, tři, čtyři,
kampak si to míří,

jedna, dvě, tři, čtyři, pět,
běží k mámě na oběd.

**Ríkejte si se mnou
(Say with me)**

František Hrubín, illustrated by
Jiří Trnka
Published by Melantrich,
Prague, 1943
This copy: 1963 Czech edition
(Albatros, Prague)
160 x 230 mm (6¼ x 9 in)

This is a collection of poems
for children by the Czech poet,
playwright and novelist Hrubín,
who was also the co-founder of
the legendary children's magazine
Mateř ídouška (The Thyme).
The poems are centred around
the simple themes of mother and
child and home life. The book is
regarded as one of the classics
of Czech children's literature.

Trnka, who died in 1969,
was one of the most inventive
and influential graphic artists to
emerge from Eastern Europe in
the twentieth century. As well as
his prolific illustration output, he
was also known for his puppetry
and animation work; he has even
been described as the 'Walt Disney
of Eastern Europe', although this
comparison is based on the level
of his popularity, rather than any
artistic or aesthetic similarity.
From 1929 to 1935, Trnka studied
at what was then the School of
Decorative Arts in Prague. His first
illustrated book was *Mr Boska the
Tiger of Vítezslaw Šmejc*, published
in 1937. In 1968 he won the
Hans Christian Andersen Award,
conferred by the International
Board on Books for Young People
(IBBY), for his lasting contribution
to children's literature.

Trnka's illustrations for *Ríkejte
si se mnou* fall just the right side of
sentimentality, and combine graphic
wit with charm and sensitivity.
Layered colours and textures with
approximate registration give a
strong lithographic feel to the page.

The integrated hand-rendered type of Gentleman's cover design reflects the author's professional involvement with both painting and design.

A Kind Welcome

'Mr. Mc.Phee, you have plenty of room up beside you for this boy.' Colin had felt too shy to ask for the coveted place beside the driver, but a rosy-faced woman, who was surrounded by well-filled shopping baskets, had somehow understood his need, and he was helped from a rear seat in the bus to one from which he could look down on the backs of the three horses, and watch the handling of the reins. Mr. Mc.Phee seemed in no hurry to be away: perhaps he hoped that all the seats would be taken; but at length he eased the brakes and the horses moved off, through narrow and winding little streets away from the sea front. Trotting at a slow pace, they left the town behind and meadows and fields appeared instead. A long, steep hill gave time to enjoy the view of an inland loch which stretched ahead between wooded banks. Scraps of conversation behind, and sometimes addressed to the driver, were mostly about the crops or the weather. Colin could see the wind and sun passing over the rich, deep grasses and was glad that the hay was not yet cut—he hoped to share in that job. Before him, in a landscape of farmland, woods and hills, was his destination, and he was happy to have arrived at last. When the bus stopped, Wallace, the

prizes differed in colour from ' Commended ' up to ' First ', making a bright patchwork pattern. They were in good time for dinner after all, and had the strawberries as a dessert, Miss Bella giving generous helpings with sugar and cream until they could eat no more. After dinner, she took Colin to see the young turkeys of which she was very proud. There were little ducks as well, and these seemed much more attractive as they sailed around the watering-pond. There was a walled-in fruit garden, with heavy laden gooseberry bushes which were not a temptation after the strawberries, but Miss Bella said Colin might visit it when tea was over. When they went indoors, the visitors had arrived, Jean and her young brother, Hugh. The children were shy of one another at first, but soon made friends. Hugh had brought a small sailing boat, so the three went down the wooded road to the sea, not far off. The tide, halfway out and ebbing, had left delightful little pools among the rocks, fine hunting places for crabs, little fish, and other sea life of that kind. Stones and weed in the water had pretty colours, like marine gardens. With bare feet and groping hands, Jean and Colin explored more crevices as the tide receded, finding many shells and selecting choice specimens to take back in pail and handkerchief, Hugh meanwhile preferring the sea for his boat, which he had safely on a string. It was with regret that they left the beach when called in for tea. It was a merry party and there were games outside afterwards. Colin was sorry when it was time to say good-bye.

The three pastel colours plus black line were drawn as separations directly on the lithographic plate by the artist.

reached, two boys, Alec and Jim, who were waiting, climbed up on the cart too. They would help with the delivering, and they squeezed on to the box-seat with Fergus and Colin. It was nice to see the bay again, the water calm and glass-like, mirroring the opposite hills. There was some traffic at the pier; one steamer had already left, her shape, blurred by the funnel's smoke, almost disappearing in the distance. The shops were still shut, many houses had a deserted air: others were all astir, doors open, knockers being polished and paths swept clean; appetising breakfast scents wafted out, postmen and newspaper boys were busy too. Alec, the older boy, stayed with the cart and horse, Jim and Colin taking the milk-cans to the customers. Jim was quick and clever. It was his habit to race to and from the houses: he could remember details of pints and payments which were still puzzling to Colin, and he was on good terms with all the dogs which guarded doors and gates. The cart kept near the sea front, making a long, slow succession of stops. It was a pleasure later, when the round was finished, to sit still again for the drive back to the town, watching the now lively scenes on shore and water. Alec and Jim said good-bye till next day, and Fergus collected the goods which Aunt Alison had ordered from the shops, Colin standing at Fanny's head, as she was impatient to be home. He looked at the interesting window displays of gifts and keepsakes, spades and pails, hooks, lines and sinkers, boats and bathing suits. When loaves, kippers and groceries were placed in the box-seat, they drove rapidly back to Brae Farm.

Tom Gentleman
Published by Transatlantic Arts,
London/New York, 1945
This copy: 1st edition
240 x 178 mm (9½ x 7 in)

Editor and publisher Noel Carrington's Transatlantic Arts venture resulted in a number of key examples in the history of picturebook printing in the UK. Carrington was particularly influential in the promotion of auto-lithographic printing (see also *High Street, Village and Town* and *Orlando*, pages 37, 45 and 63). *Brae Farm* was the only picturebook written and illustrated by Tom Gentleman; by the end of the century, his son, David Gentleman (see page 121), would be far better known as a designer and illustrator. But this book has a very special period charm and an intimacy that comes from the author not only having written and illustrated it, but also having been closely involved in the print process, working directly on the lithographic plates. The story tells of a small boy, Colin, who is sent to holiday alone on an idyllic Scottish island, where he helps out on a farm. The book is rooted in Gentleman's own Scottish upbringing.

After studying painting at the Glasgow School of Art, Gentleman moved with his wife to London to seek design work to augment his meagre income from selling paintings. He found work with the advertising agencies Benson's and Crawford's. Later, he worked for the famous Shell design studio, under the legendary Jack Beddington, where he designed posters alongside such greats as Edward McKnight Kauffer and Ashley Havinden. But, as his son David recalls, 'he'd rather have been a painter pure and simple.'[1]

1 *Artwork*, by David Gentleman (Ebury Press, London, 2002).

Coarse wartime paper lends texture to the illustrations.

Enid Marx
Published by Faber & Faber,
London, 1945
This copy: 1st edition
155 x 240 mm (6 x 9½ in)

A distant relative of Karl Marx, Enid was first and foremost a pattern maker. She designed seating fabrics for London Transport, wrapping papers and laminates for wartime furniture. A recipient of the prestigious title of Royal Designer for Industry, she was also a lifelong collector of folk art and ephemera, and, along with her close friend Margaret Lambert, wrote *English Popular Art* (Batsford, 1951), a key text on the everyday arts.

Marx was known for her energy and outspokenness; even when well into her nineties, she wrote regularly to Sir Christopher Frayling, then Rector of the Royal College of Art, with advice on the best way to do things. Marx herself had been a student at the RCA in the early 1920s, along with Edward Bawden and Eric Ravilious in the group that their tutor, Paul Nash, famously described as 'an outbreak of talent' (see pages 37 and 109). Despite failing her diploma, Marx soon began to make a name for herself designing textiles.

Book illustration was one of Marx's many and wide-ranging activities, and her few self-authored picturebooks are now scarce and highly collectable; these include a selection of titles with wartime themes, such as *Bulgy the Barrage Balloon*, *The Pigeon Ace* and *Nelson, the Kite of the King's Navy*. *Little White Bear* was lithographed at the Baynard Press, with the pages alternating between two- and three-colour separations. Marx's fragile draughtsmanship is compensated for by sheer spirit and pattern.

The extreme landscape format of the book is exploited by Marx as she stretches the whale to make the most of the shape.

Vuoi sapere come mai questi tre uccellini: CIÒ, CIÀ e CÌ, si trovano in gabbia? Te lo farò raccontare da loro.

CIÀ

passò Carletto e mi raccolse. Povero uccellino! disse, vieni con me che ti curerò e ti farò guarire. Ed ora eccomi qui in gabbia, guarito ma non posso più volare come prima dentro al mio grande albero.

CIÒ

CÌ

Vuoi sapere come mai questi tre uccellini: CIÒ, CIÀ e CÌ, si trovano in gabbia? Te lo farò raccontare da loro.

CIÀ

Io non ho storie da raccontare.
Sono nato in gabbia.

CÌ

A Munari book is a complete experience that allows the reader to engage with its physical form from multiple directions and viewpoints.

BRUNO MUNARI

storie di tre uccellini

CORRAINI EDITORE

22
Storie di tre uccellini (A tale of three little birds)

Bruno Munari
Published by Mondadori,
Verona, 1945
This copy: 2007 Italian edition
(Corraini, Mantua)
320 x 240 mm (12½ x 9½ in)

Bruno Munari's contribution to the evolution of the picturebook is inestimable. He made many books for children, alongside his richly varied life as an artist and designer, or, more properly, as an artist-designer. He was initially part of the Italian Futurist movement as an artist and exhibited his work widely, but he refused to be tied down to the idea of art as a separate activity from the design of everyday things. In his 1971 book *Design as Art*, Munari outlined his Bauhaus-inspired views on the need for art and everyday life to be much more closely aligned. He felt that artists should not be elevated or celebrated as stars, but should be engaged in the design of such things as shop signs and food mixers. His treatise has recently been republished, and his theories and ideas seem as relevant today as they did in the early 1970s.

Munari enjoyed playing with the structure of a book and its relationship to content. *Storie di tre uccellini* is a typically playful book-within-a-book and story-within-a-story. He would never allow himself to be wedded to any idea of personal 'style', preferring always to let content dictate form instead. Many of his books have now been republished by Edizioni Corraini.

Vuoi sapere come mai questi tre uccellini: CIÒ, CIÀ e CÌ, si trovano in gabbia? Te lo farò raccontare da loro.

CIÀ

Quando mi svegliai vidi un uomo con una gran barba nera. Mi guardò. Pianse. Che ne sarà di me? Pensai, e poi mi addormentai.

CIÒ

CÌ

– Lo vuoi un fenicottero tutto rivestito
di piume rosse? È un bellissimo
animale e lo puoi tenere in anticamera.

– No. Non lo voglio perché fuma la
pipa. Dammi un'altra bestia.

– Lo vuoi u
di piume
animale c

– No. Non
pipa. Da

– Vuoi l'istrice? Lo puoi tenere in terrazza
ed è bellissimo con la neve.

– Non lo voglio perché è un brontolone.

**Il venditore di animali
(Animals for sale)**

Bruno Munari
Published by Mondadori,
Verona, 1945
This copy: 2004 Italian edition
(Corraini, Mantua)
320 x 240 mm (12½ x 9½ in)

Munari is again in playful mood
with *Il venditore di animali*, one
of a series of nine picturebooks
published in 1945, including *Storie
di tre uccellini* (see page 53). In
1986 Munari reflected on his early
children's books: 'In 1945 my son
was five and I was wondering: are
there books that are just right for
children? Books they really like?
How can we make the reader the
real "main character" in the book?
I tried making a few and children
still like these books a lot today.
I get wonderful letters.'

The resulting outpouring of
experimental books has left a
lasting legacy, alongside Munari's
other writings, which provide a
model for the creation and academic
study of design. 'The designer
today re-establishes the long-lost
contact between art and the public,
between living people and art as
a living thing.'

– Vuoi l'armadillo? si arrotola come
una palla e lo puoi tenere nel cassetto
del comò.

– Non lo voglio perché ogni sera
l'armadillo torna a casa un poco brillo.

– Lo vuoi u...
di piume...
animale ...

– No. Non ...
pipa. Dai

hat on for breakfast made of roses. She
kissed Ella and said, "My dear little girl,
here is some salad for your meal and afterwards you may have your presents." Ella
swallowed her salad hastily. Then she
went with her Mama to the drawing room
to see her presents. Ella was delighted
with all her gifts. Her mama let her stay

The simplicity and strength of Swanwick's compositions make them perfectly suited to the tiny scale of the book.

Mary was Ella's particular friend. After tea they all played postman's knock and leapfrog. No one could leap over Ella because she was so tall for her age. At six o'clock Ella's friends departed and Ella was allowed to have dinner with her Mama, Papa and Grandmother because it was her birthday. She was also allowed a small glass of champagne which made her smack her lips. After dinner her mama played the piano and sang. She had a beautiful voice trained in Italy. During her Mama's performance, Ella knelt on her chair and looked out of the window at the palm trees

at home as it was her birthday and she took Ella shopping in the morning, and they had an expensive ice-cream each at a Giraffe bazaar in the town. The tables

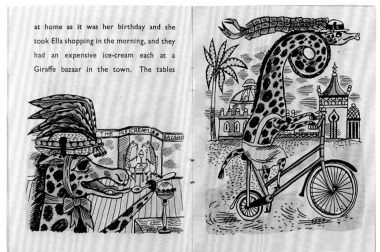

24
Ella's Birthday

Betty Swanwick
Published by Transatlantic Arts, London, 1946
This copy: 1st edition
130 x 100 mm (5 x 4 in)

Number 42 in the tiny-format Bantam Picture Book series, this is another book from the various publishing imprints for which we have to thank the great Noel Carrington (see page 45).

Betty Swanwick was a highly original, perhaps eccentric, British artist. She studied at Goldsmiths, where tutor Edward Bawden (see page 109) recognized and encouraged her exceptional talent; she later returned to teach illustration at the college as Bawden's successor. She also studied at the Central School of Art and the Royal College of Art. By the time she left art school, Swanwick was in demand as a designer and illustrator, most notably producing a series of wonderful posters for London Transport.

Swanwick described herself as 'part of a small tradition of English painting that is a bit eccentric, a little odd and a little visionary'.[1] The drawings and paintings that she concentrated her energies on in later life could certainly be described as visionary, flowing from an English tradition that may be traced back through Stanley Spencer to Samuel Palmer and William Blake.

Swanwick's book work included several 'illustrated novelettes', which she wrote and illustrated herself, the best known of which is *The Cross Purposes* (Editions Poetry London, 1945). The Bantam books are now extremely rare. *Ella's Birthday*, one of two that she produced in the series, demonstrates Swanwick's wonderful economy of line and assured use of space. It is printed letterpress in four-colour separations.

1 *Betty Swanwick: Artist and Visionary*, by Paddy Rossmore (Chris Beetles Ltd, London, 2008).

shake out the
leg, and it made
e that he *could*
to stir up his

and have their
rpment of grey
hich a chain of
ear fell in suc-
s just beginning
uch to Sandy's
and various; he
hem tied in his

ly said to Ellen,
es, I *must* Ellen,
. Ellen sat and
papers with her
ed to buy some
his legs already
e called:

hem rocks and
he didn't seem
flannel shorts
orbed.

and answered,

Odo Cross, illustrated by
John Minton
Published by John Lehmann,
London, 1947
This copy: 1st edition
255 x 190 mm (10 x 7½ in)

During the period immediately
following World War II, a certain
mood characterized the arts in
Britain for a decade or so, which
has since been labelled 'Neo-
Romantic'. It was distinguished by
what some have described as an
inward-looking return to landscape,
a sense of place and the spirit
of nature. Such artists as John
Craxton, Keith Vaughan, Michael
Ayrton, John Piper and especially
John Minton looked back to Samuel
Palmer and William Blake for
inspiration, immersing themselves
in a kind of elegiac, mournful, at
times overwrought visual language.
One of the lasting legacies of the
period is the crossover that took
place between gallery art and
book illustration, creating within
a few short years a number of key
twentieth-century illustrated books.
At the forefront of this movement
was the publisher John Lehmann,
who commissioned many of these
artists to work with leading writers
and poets of the period.

Minton was not a natural
children's book illustrator, and this
was the only one of his books that
fell into that category. (He had been
introduced to Paul Odo Cross
by Lehmann, and later stayed with
him in Jamaica, a visit that inspired
some of Minton's best paintings.)
The book is illustrated with eight
three-colour illustrations and
numerous black-and-white line
drawings. These and the wrap-
around dust jacket are redolent with
the motifs and mannerisms that
would become Minton's trademarks
– winding lanes, reclining figures
and mournful moons.

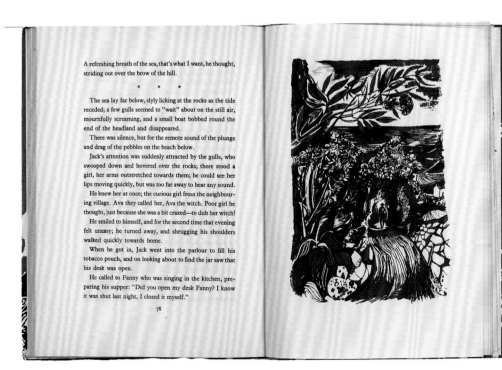

A refreshing breath of the sea, that's what I want, he thought, striding out over the brow of the hill.

* * * *

The sea lay far below, slyly licking at the rocks as the tide receded; a few gulls seemed to "wait" about on the still air, mournfully screaming, and a small boat bobbed round the end of the headland and disappeared.

There was silence, but for the remote sound of the plunge and drag of the pebbles on the beach below.

Jack's attention was suddenly attracted by the gulls, who swooped down and hovered over the rocks; there stood a girl, her arms outstretched towards them; he could see her lips moving quickly, but was too far away to hear any sound.

He knew her at once; the curious girl from the neighbouring village. Ava they called her, Ava the witch. Poor girl he thought, just because she was a bit crazed—to dub her witch!

He smiled to himself, and for the second time that evening felt uneasy; he turned away, and shrugging his shoulders walked quickly towards home.

When he got in, Jack went into the parlour to fill his tobacco pouch, and on looking about to find the jar saw that his desk was open.

He called to Fanny who was singing in the kitchen, preparing his supper: "Did you open my desk Fanny? I know it was shut last night, I closed it myself."

78

There was once a King who had twelve daughters, each more beautiful than the other. They slept together in a hall where their beds stood close to one another, and at night, when they had gone to bed, the King ordered the door to be locked and bolted.

But when he unlocked the door the next morning, he discovered that their shoes had been quite danced into holes and no one could tell how it happened.

As with all Picture Puffins of the time, colour spreads alternate with those in black and white. This meant the entire book could be printed on one giant sheet of paper.

On the opposite side of the lake stood a splendid brightly lit castle

So the King sent out a proclamation, saying, that anyone who could find out where the princesses did their nights dancing should choose one of them to be his wife and should reign after his death. But whoever tried and failed to make the discovery after three days and nights was to forfeit his life.
A Prince soon presented himself and offered to take the risk of losing his head.

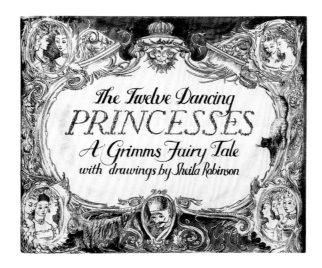

Although the artwork was created as a single finished piece, it looks as though it has been produced using separations. This is due to Robinson's dry-brush technique for applying watercolour and ink.

Sheila Robinson
Self-published student project, hand-drawn and hand-bound, late 1940s
This copy: Posthumously published by the Centre for Children's Book Studies, Anglia Ruskin University, Cambridge, 2012
180 x 220 mm (7 x 8¾ in)

Sheila Robinson studied under Edward Bawden (see page 109) at London's Royal College of Art in the late 1940s before going on to work across a wide range of disciplines, such as book illustration, printmaking, exhibition design and other areas of three-dimensional design, including that of seaside amusement-park rides. She also contributed various designs to the Festival of Britain, the great 1951 jamboree of British postwar design confidence.

Robinson settled in Great Bardfield in Essex, along with a small group of artists who followed Bawden and Eric Ravilious to the village, creating a loose 'community' of artists who would exhibit their work in their homes every summer. The work of these artists is well represented in the collections of the Fry Art Gallery and Museum in the nearby town of Saffron Walden. It is here that the original handmade and hand-bound copy of Robinson's *Twelve Dancing Princesses* resides.

Produced when Robinson was a student, more than 60 years ago, the book is based on the Brothers Grimm fairy tale of the same name, and was designed to the format of the Picture Puffins of the time (see *Village and Town* by S. R. Badmin, page 45). For whatever reason, it was never published during her lifetime. In order to publish it in 2012, it was necessary to use Photoshop to correct much of the misspelled hand lettering. This edition also includes a dust jacket that shows some of the sketchbook research for the project, also held at the Fry.

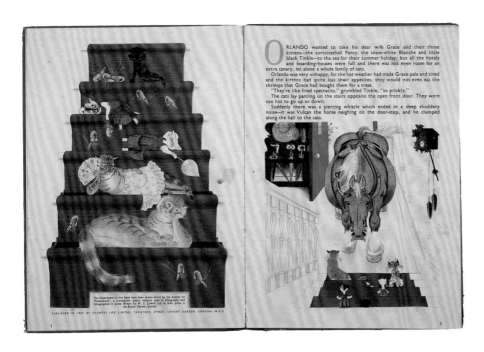

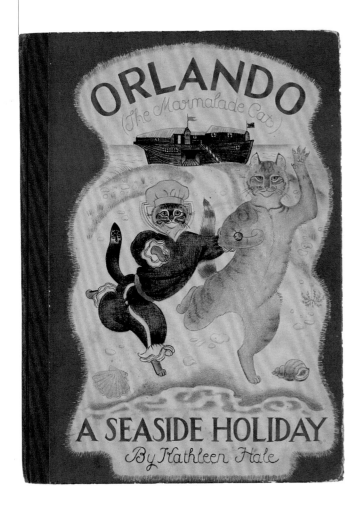

Orlando: A Seaside Holiday features Hale's typically exuberant, idiosyncratic humour, and rather chaotic and inconsistent draughtsmanship, design and characterization.

The colours sing on the page and the book exudes charm and a sense of place, the latter clearly being the Suffolk seaside town of Aldeburgh (renamed Owlbarrow).

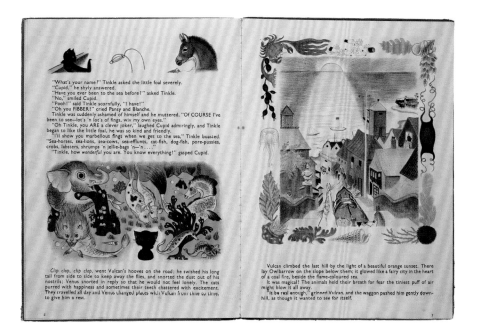

Orlando (The Marmalade Cat): A Seaside Holiday

Kathleen Hale
Published by Country Life,
London, 1952
This copy: 1st edition
357 x 260 mm (14 x 10¼ in)

A serendipitous coming together of three key figures in British book illustration was behind the emergence of the highly popular, iconic and long-running Orlando series. The three were artist-author Kathleen Hale, publisher Noel Carrington of Country Life (and Transatlantic Arts) and the printer Geoffrey Smith at W. S. Cowell of Ipswich. As Ruth Artmonsky recounts in her history of this important printer, the three came together at an opportune moment in the development of children's picturebooks.[1]

Hale had tried to get her first Orlando ideas published via a literary agent with no success. Being already acquainted with Smith, a meeting between the three parties was arranged. This was at a time when Carrington was developing a keen interest in auto-lithographic methods (see also *Village and Town* and *Brae Farm*, pages 45 and 49). The first Orlando book, *Orlando: A Camping Holiday*, was published in 1938. With such a large format, the process of colour separation from Hale's detailed originals by Cowell's technicians proved expensive. So Hale learnt to do the separations herself, working closely with the printers and taking the lithographic plates home to work on. *Orlando: A Trip Abroad* quickly followed.

There were many Orlando titles over the years, in both large and smaller format, the latter including some early titles under Carrington's hugely popular and long-running Puffin Picture Book imprint. Later titles were published under the John Murray imprint, Harlequin – also edited by Carrington.

1 *Do You Want it Good or Do You Want it Tuesday – The Halcyon Days of W. S. Cowell Ltd. Printers*, by Ruth Artmonsky (Artmonsky Arts, London, 2011).

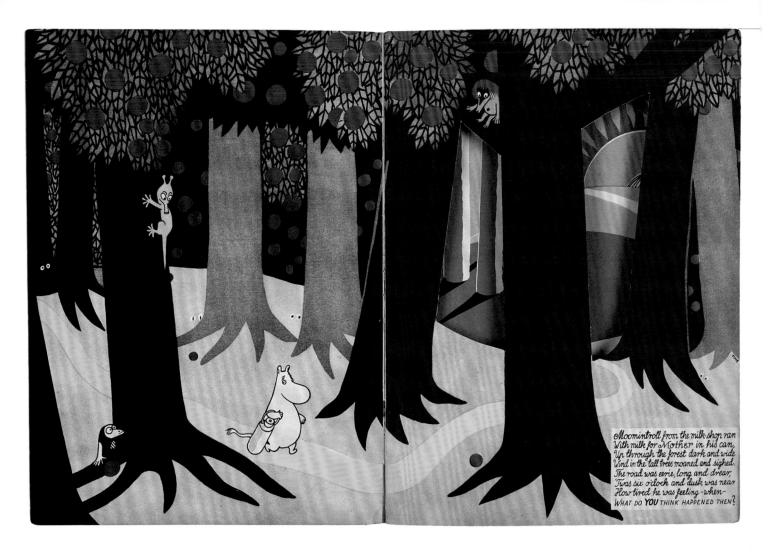

Moomintroll from the milk-shop ran
With milk for Mother in his can,
Up through the forest dark and wide.
Wind in the tall trees moaned and sighed.
The road was eerie, long and dreary,
'Twas six o'clock and dusk was near.
How tired he was feeling—when—
WHAT DO **YOU** THINK HAPPENED THEN?

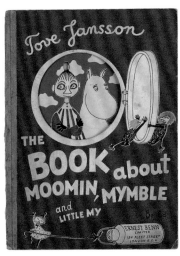

Tove Jansson

THE
BOOK about
MOOMIN, MYMBLE
and LITTLE MY

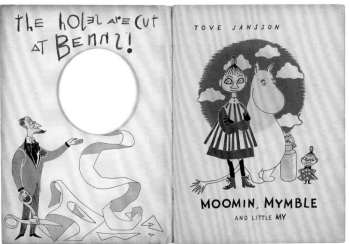

THE hOlEs are cut
at Benn2!

TOVE JANSSON

MOOMIN, MYMBLE
AND LITTLE MY

Alas!!!
The milk she could not
For it had curdled and
She said 'Now, in the f
Drink strawberry juice a

Cut-out sections throughout
the book give the reader forward
and backward glimpses
through time and space.

28
The Book About Moomin, Mymble and Little My

Tove Jansson
Published by Ernest Benn,
London, 1953
This copy: 1st edition
288 x 212 mm (11¼ x 8¼ in)

The artist and writer Tove Jansson
created a unique, idiosyncratic
world that has permeated
numerous cultures and all age
groups since the first Moomin book,
The Moomins and the Great Flood,
appeared in 1945. Jansson was
born in 1914 to an artistic family
belonging to the Swedish-speaking
minority in Finland; her mother was
a graphic designer and illustrator,
her father a sculptor. In the 1930s
Jansson studied art in Stockholm,
then at the Finnish Academy of Fine
Arts and finally at the École des
Beaux-Arts in Paris. Before writing
and illustrating her first book,
during World War II, she produced
illustrations for books, magazines
and posters, as well as satirical
cartoon strips.

It has been said that the Moomin
characters and their overall ethos
were inspired by the bohemian,
liberal values of Jansson's own family
and upbringing. She was awarded
the Hans Christian Andersen
Award in 1966 for her outstanding
contribution to children's literature,
and the Moomin Valley Museum
in the city of Tampere, Finland, now
houses around 2,000 exhibits.

*The Book About Moomin,
Mymble and Little My* was the first
of only five Moomin picturebooks.
In it, Moomintroll travels through
the woods to bring home milk for
Moominmama. But encounters with
other characters from the Moomin
world, such as the Fillijonks and
Hattifatteners, cause us to question
whether Moomin will ever complete
her journey.

An early example of the use of type as image: the loudspeaker announcements are arranged to convey sound.

Craigie's flat-colour illustrations were created as line-block separations with no overprinting.

In London it snowed and snowed and snowed. No planes could fly, but the Little Steamroller went on rolling and rolling. "Up my hearty," said Bill Driver. "We want to finish this stretch by Christmas," and the Little Steamrolle through the storm which meant "Wh snow?" The great airliners did.

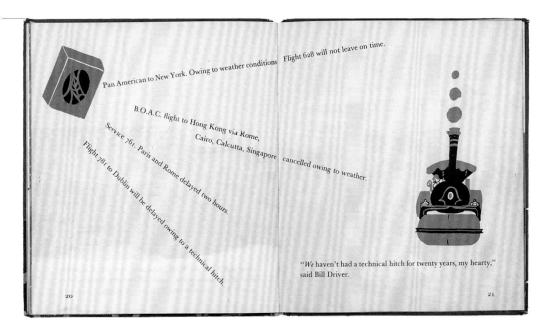

Pan American to New York. Owing to weather conditions Flight 628 will not leave on time.

B.O.A.C. flight to Hong Kong via Rome, Cairo, Calcutta, Singapore cancelled owing to weather.

Service 761. Paris and Rome delayed two hours.

Flight 781 to Dublin will be delayed owing to a technical hitch.

"*We* haven't had a technical hitch for twenty years, my hearty," said Bill Driver.

20

21

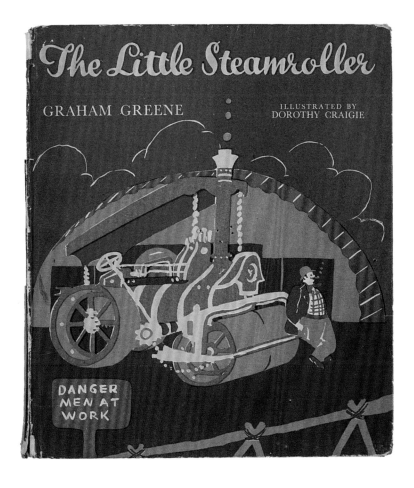

ff of smoke
ut a bit of

29
The Little Steamroller

Graham Greene, illustrated by
Dorothy Craigie
Published by Max Parrish,
London, 1953
This copy: 1st edition
220 x 190 mm (8¾ x 7½ in)

Dorothy Glover was working as a costume designer in the theatre when she met the celebrated novelist Graham Greene in 1938. She adopted the pen name Dorothy Craigie for her book illustration work, and collaborated with Greene (with whom she was having an affair) on several picturebooks. This was the last book that they produced together, and Greene's fourth and final book for children.

The Little Steamroller tells the unlikely tale of the heroic exploits of a London Airport-based steamroller in thwarting and capturing a gang of smugglers. Craigie was clearly not a great draughtsman, but her picturebooks with Greene have considerable period charm. She worked entirely in flat colours, presumably created as separations, which give the effect of screen-printing. There is no attempt to convey spacial depth or to limit the number of colours on any one page. Riotous full-colour pages alternate with spreads printed in two colours: blue and grey.

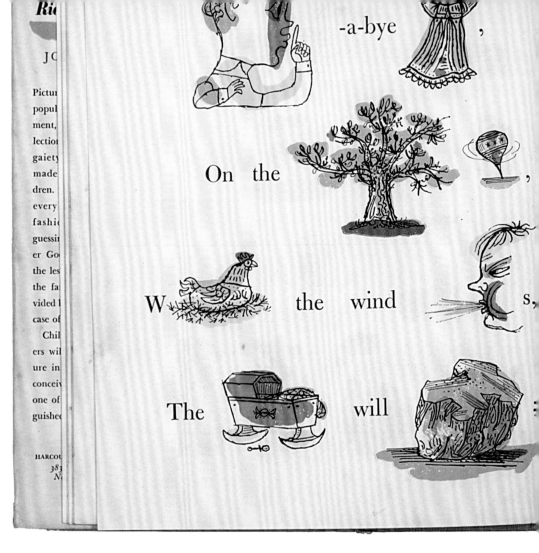

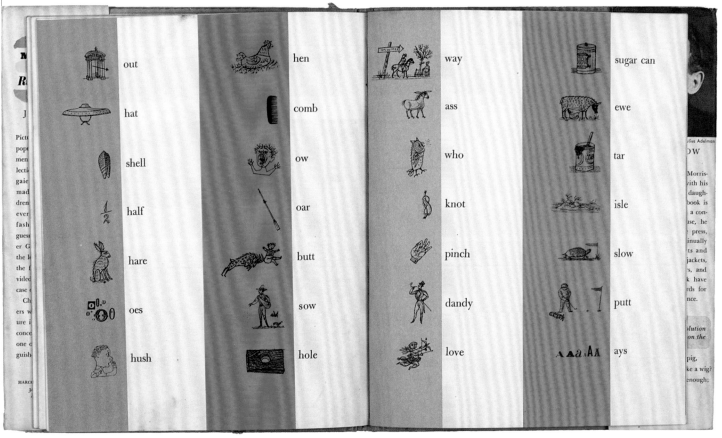

W   the   breaks,

The   will

WILL

30
Mother Goose Riddle Rhymes

Joseph Low
('with help from Ruth Low')
Published by Harcourt,
Brace & Co., New York, 1953
This copy: 1st edition
220 x 185 mm (8¾ x 7¼ in)

Joseph Low died in 2007 at the age of 95, after a long and varied career as a graphic artist. Although children's picturebooks formed a substantial part of his output for many years, he also produced designs for album covers, books and magazines, including the *New Yorker*, from 1940. Low also founded his own private press, having acquired a vintage hand press from a newspaper that had closed down. He named the venture Eden Hill Press, after the road in Newtown, Connecticut, on which he lived with his wife Ruth. From there, Low produced a number of signed, limited-edition books over which he had complete control (design, illustration and printing) – a forerunner perhaps of the kind of activities in which today's authorial illustrators are increasingly engaged.

In *Mother Goose Riddle Rhymes*, Low takes a selection of Mother Goose rhymes and presents them as picture puzzles or rebuses for children to unravel, with pictures of objects or activities replacing words. Using five colours as multi-plate separations with playfully approximate registration, the artist creates pattern and movement across the page. Low's work is often compared to that of Saul Steinberg and Ben Shahn (see page 83), but there is more than a hint of the dry visual wit of Edward Bawden (see page 109) here too.

Elements of Low's interior illustrations are extracted and repeated to create patterned paper designs for the cover boards.

Mr. McGregor came up with
a sieve, which he intended
to pop upon the top of Peter.
But Peter wriggled out
just in time,
leaving his jacket behind,
and rushed into
the tool shed,
and jumped into a can.
It would have been
a beautiful thing
to hide in,
if it had not had
so much water in it.

McGregor. Now run along and don't get into mischief. I am going out."

Then old Mrs. Rabbit took a basket and her umbrella, and went through the wood to the baker's. She bought a loaf of brown bread and five currant buns.

Flopsy, Mopsy, and Cotton-tail, who were good little bunnies, went down the lane to gather blackberries. But Peter, who was very naughty, ran straight away to Mr. McGregor's garden and squeezed under the gate!

First he ate some lettuces and some French beans, and then he ate some radishes. And then, feeling rather sick, he went to look for some parsley.

31
Peter Rabbit

Beatrix Potter, illustrated by
Leonard Weisgard
Published by Grosset & Dunlap,
New York, 1955
This copy: 1st edition
290 x 236 mm (11½ x 9¼ in)

One of the more prolific American illustrators of the twentieth century, Weisgard worked on more than 200 books, and is particularly remembered for his collaborations with the author Margaret Wise Brown. He was born in Newhaven, Connecticut, but the family lived in England (his father's birthplace) until Weisgard was 8, when they moved back to the US. The children's literature critic and commentator Leonard Marcus has observed that Weisgard was one of the artists who 'reinvented the American picturebook'. He was certainly an innovator who experimented with a wide range of media to create distinctively vibrant graphic effects. In particular, it was his use of stencilling and spongeing that brought such a range of textures and shapes to the page.

Here, Weisgard takes Beatrix Potter's iconic tale of Peter Rabbit's adventure in Mr McGregor's garden and translates it into picturebook format. Mr McGregor himself is transformed into a 1950s gardener, and the young rabbits are similarly updated. The adventure takes place against a backdrop of rich colour and pattern, exemplified by the theatrical cover design.

In later life, Weisgard and his family moved to Denmark, where his children continue to live. He died in 2000.

A quiet, single-colour motif on the cover boards contrasts with the busy dust-jacket design.

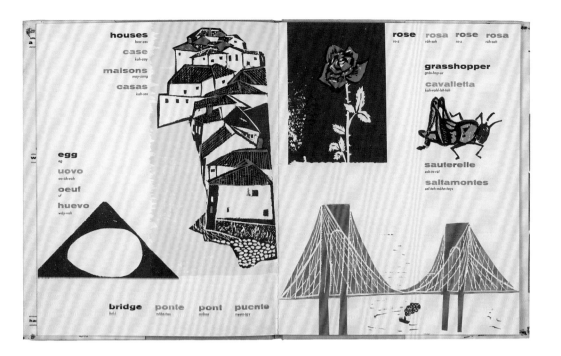

32

See and Say: A Picture Book in Four Languages

Antonio Frasconi
Published by Harcourt,
Brace & Co., New York, 1955
This copy: 1st edition
265 x 215 mm (10½ x 8½ in)

Often described as a master of the woodcut, Antonio Frasconi died in January 2013 at the age of 93. He was drawn to the medium after seeing the work of Paul Gauguin in an exhibition of French Impressionists and post-Impressionists. Born in Buenos Aires to parents of Italian descent, he was brought up in Uruguay and moved to New York after World War II, having received a scholarship to the Art Students League. Throughout his working life, Frasconi placed great importance on the social, political and ethical perspective of making art, and is particularly known for his anti-Fascist posters.

See and Say was created as a book to help young children learn basic words in four languages. It was inspired by Frasconi's experience of growing up in an Italian-speaking household, while needing to speak Spanish at school. As he writes on the copyright page: 'The idea that there are many nationalities speaking many languages is to me one of the most important for a child to understand.'

The book uses four colours (black, blue, red and yellow), each representing one of the four languages when used in the text. In the images, the raw, expressive nature of the crudely cut wood and the texture of its grain combine with meticulously planned overprinting of the four colours to expand the palette.

Overprinting of transparent colours creates subtle hues whilst retaining the grain of the wood.

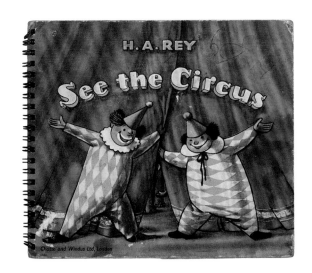

Ted has a tricycle,
 so very small,
He cannot ride it
 because he's so tall.

If you want to find out
 WHO the rider will be,
Just open the flap,
 and then you will see.

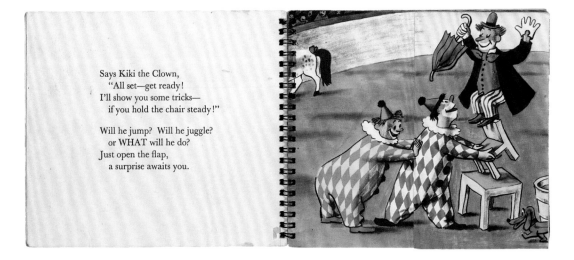

Says Kiki the Clown,
 "All set—get ready!
I'll show you some tricks—
 if you hold the chair steady!"

Will he jump? Will he juggle?
 or WHAT will he do?
Just open the flap,
 a surprise awaits you.

The Reys' much-loved monkeys make a surprise appearance.

33

See the Circus

H. A. Rey
Published by Houghton Mifflin
Company, Boston, 1955
This copy: later undated UK edition
(Chatto & Windus, London)
140 x 160 mm (5½ x 6¼ in)

Margret and Hans Rey are best
known for the enduringly successful
Curious George series. The two
worked together and married in
Rio de Janeiro, having both grown
up in Hamburg. The story of their
epic escape on bicycles from the
Nazi occupation of France in World
War II is told in Louise Borden's
*The Journey That Saved Curious
George*.[1]

See the Circus is one of three
small 'lift the flap' books that Rey
designed in the 1950s, and which
have been reprinted in the years
since. The others were *Anybody
at Home?* and *Feed the Animals*.
The series is designed to a simple
formula of an extended page that
is folded into the book, and which
needs to be opened to reveal a
hidden element referred to in the
facing text. As we observe the
tightrope, we read:
　　Will someone walk on it?
　　WHO will it be?
　　Just open the flap,
　　And then you will see.
The drama, theatre and colour of
the circus is heightened by this
basic form of interaction between
young child and book.

**The unfolding and extending
of the page extends time and
creates a mini-narrative on
each page.**

he Clown,
—get ready!
u some tricks—
d the chair steady!"

ip? Will he juggle?
T will he do?
ie flap,
 awaits you.

1　*The Journey That Saved Curious
　George*, by Louise Borden, illustrated
　by Allan Drummond (Houghton Mifflin
　Company, Boston, 2005).

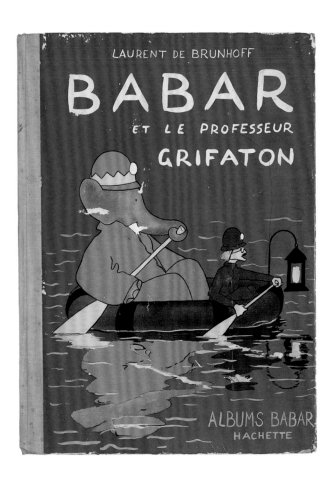

BABAR
ET LE PROFESSEUR
GRIFATON

LAURENT DE BRUNHOFF

ALBUMS BABAR
HACHETTE

Ils glissent
au milieu de stalactites et de voûtes ténébreuses. Tout à coup u
immense statue sort de l'ombre. « C'est la statue du roi des mammou
b...ie Arthur. La vieille dame nous a raconté son histoire à l'éco

Les voilà ! Tout le monde est content. Le professeur Grifaton est très ému : il a tellement entendu parler de Babar et de Céleste par sa sœur. Babar embrasse la vieille dame de bon cœur. Pom, Flore et Alexandre sont ravis de connaître leurs nouveaux amis. Quant à la voiture, elle a beaucoup de succès auprès des éléphants.

4

5

The author fully exploits the large scale of the book with dramatic double-page-spread images.

The de Brunhoffs' world of elephants living an entirely normal, bourgeois human existence is somehow instantly believable.

Restés seuls un instant, Babar, Céleste et la vieille dame voient revenir les éléphants déguisés: c'est

une surprise organisée par Nadine qui a trouvé des costumes dans les armoires du Palais des Fêtes!

.12.   .13.

34

Babar et le professeur Grifaton (Babar and Professor Grifaton)

Laurent de Brunhoff
Published by Hachette, Paris, 1956
This copy: 1st edition
365 x 265 mm (14¼ x 10½ in)

The original Babar was created by Laurent de Brunhoff's father, Jean. He was a painter, and had based his character on the bedside stories that his wife, Cécile, told to Laurent and his brother, Mathieu, as children. The first of Jean de Brunhoff's published Babar books appeared in 1931 – *Histoire de Babar* (*The Story of Babar*). Very large in format, and beautifully drawn and printed, there had been nothing like it before and it was an immediate success. It was the first of six Babar books to be published throughout the 1930s, but Jean died of tuberculosis in 1937, with the books at the height of their popularity, and Laurent only 12 years old.

After World War II, Laurent studied art at the Académie de la Grande Chaumière and decided to take on the mantle of his father's work; he published his first Babar book, *Babar et ce coquin d'Arthur* (*Babar's Cousin: That Rascal Arthur*), in 1946 at the age of 21. He has continued the work throughout his life, creating more than 30 additional Babar titles over the last 60 years. Asked in 1974 why Babar has remained so popular with children, he replied: 'Different things: first, an elephant is very popular, because at the same time it's funny and because of the trunk, and then the big, big fat animal is somehow reassuring – children feel security with him … The most bizarre things are presented just as normal … An elephant going on the river in a hat for instance, it is completely silly and crazy, and yet it is not.'[1]

1   *The Pied Pipers: Interviews with the Influential Creators of Children's Literature*, edited by Justin Wintle and Emma Fisher (Paddington Press, New York, 1975).

and a leaf be a ferry
for a snail.

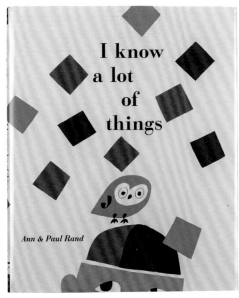

I know
a lot
of
things

Ann & Paul Rand

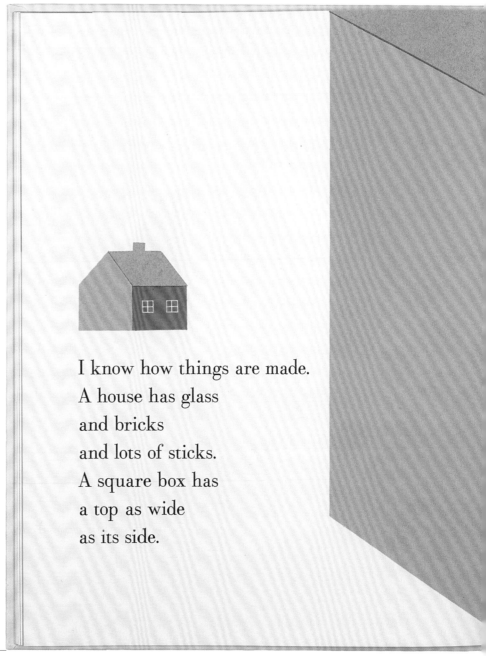

I know how things are made.
A house has glass
and bricks
and lots of sticks.
A square box has
a top as wide
as its side.

and climb a tree
high as the sky
to watch a bird fly by
and an acorn drop
kerplop kerplop

Ann and Paul Rand
Published by Harcourt,
Brace & Co., New York, 1956
This copy: 2009 US edition
(Chronicle Books, San Francisco)
260 x 210 mm (10¼ x 8¼ in)

It has been suggested that the first act of brand-identity creation that the legendary graphic designer Paul Rand undertook was that of changing his name from Peretz Rosenbaum. Rand's career and influence on modern graphic design have been well documented. The son of a grocer, he was brought up in an Orthodox Jewish family in Brooklyn and studied at the Pratt Institute (1929–32), the Parsons School of Design (1932–33) and the Art Students League (1933–34). He took inspiration from European avant-garde graphic design and claimed to be 'largely self-taught as a designer, learning about the works of Cassandre and Moholy-Nagy from European magazines such as *Gebrauchsgraphik*'.[1] Rand's unique approach also permeated his work as Professor of Graphic Design at Yale from 1956 to 1985.

I Know a Lot of Things was the first of four picturebooks made by Rand and his wife, Ann, the others being *Sparkle and Spin* (1957), *Little 1* (1962) and *Listen! Listen!* (1970). Ann Rand's words seem tailor-made for Paul's graphic vision, the two complementing each other with apparently effortless economy. Paul Rand uses his trademark bold cut-out shapes to describe simple visual concepts from a child's perspective. Text is always treated as a visual element and, wherever possible, is integrated as a pictorial element so that reading words and reading pictures becomes a single, inseparable process.

1 'Tribute: Paul Rand 1914–1996', by Michael Bierut, in *ID* magazine (Jan/Feb, 1997).

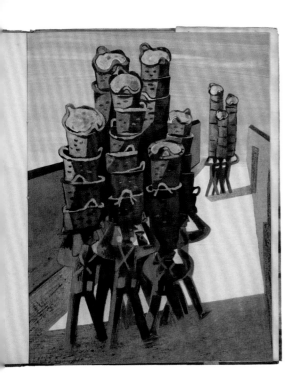

Le Witt's formalizing of shapes and colours is in tune with the Surrealist and neo-Romantic mood of the time.

There are echoes of Surrealists such as Giorgio de Chirico in the two-colour pages that alternate with full-colour printing.

The **Vegetabull**

STORY AND PICTURES

Jan Le Witt

Collins

Jan Le Witt
Published by Collins, London, 1956
This copy: 1st edition
280 x 215 mm (11 x 8½ in)

Le Witt is perhaps best known as one half of the highly successful design partnership Lewitt-Him, which he formed with fellow Polish émigré George Him. This was a partnership that lasted for 20 years, despite their very different, sometimes clashing personalities.[1] Of the two, Him was the trained graphic designer, while Le Witt had ambitions to be a painter (which he later became). As well as their widely published work in advertising and poster design, the two were responsible for a number of children's picturebooks. Perhaps one of the best known of these was the first book in the Little Red Engine series, *The Little Red Engine Gets a Name*, written by Diana Ross. Subsequent titles in the series were illustrated by Leslie Wood. The pair also wrote and illustrated *The Football's Revolt* (Country Life, 1939), and collaborated with Le Witt's wife, Alina, on *Blue Peter* (Faber & Faber, 1943) and *Five Silly Cats* (Minerva, 1944).

The Vegetabull was one of the first projects that Le Witt pursued after the dissolution of the partnership in 1955. Le Witt had designed sets for Sadler's Wells Ballet in London, and this highly theatrical book, redolent with the motifs and patterns of the time, is a pure 1950s period piece. Across the pages of the book there are clear echoes of many of the British artists of that period, including John Minton, John Tunnard, Keith Vaughan and Prunella Clough.

Right in the middle of the vast ocean, there was an island called Mandolia.

Once each year S.S. Barbarossa, the mail boat, came from far away to deliver the mail and bring supplies. And whenever the Barbarossa anchored, her crew went ashore to look at the two most amazing things on the island.

First there was the Mandolia tree, for which the island had been named, the one and only tree in the whole world growing mandolins.

Then there was the fabulous Great Wall. Above it strange figures towered: eighty-eight knights in shining armour, entangled in a web of wires and moving at a whim of the wind.

"What is behind the Great Wall?" the sailors would ask.

"Our vegetable garden," the islanders replied, and went on mending their nets.

1   *Jan Le Witt and George Him*, by Ruth Artmonsky (Design series, Antique Collectors' Club, Suffolk, England, 2008).

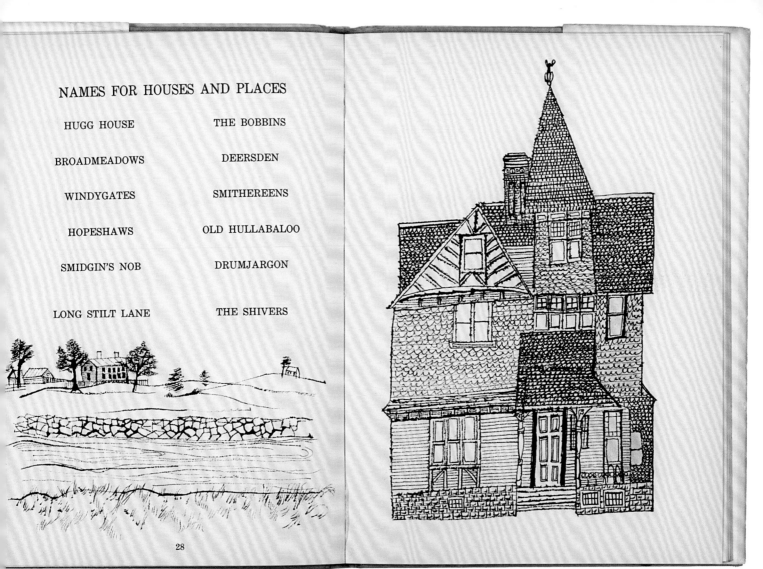

NAMES FOR HOUSES AND PLACES

HUGG HOUSE	THE BOBBINS
BROADMEADOWS	DEERSDEN
WINDYGATES	SMITHEREENS
HOPESHAWS	OLD HULLABALOO
SMIDGIN'S NOB	DRUMJARGON
LONG STILT LANE	THE SHIVERS

28

Shahn's typography and
illustrations never overpower
Reid's text; rather, they support
and augment the words.

Reid's text takes a poet's
delight in the sounds that
words make.

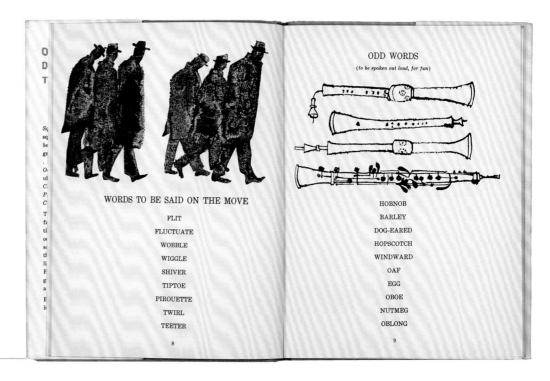

ODD WORDS
(to be spoken out loud, for fun)

WORDS TO BE SAID ON THE MOVE

FLIT	HOBNOB
FLUCTUATE	BARLEY
WOBBLE	DOG-EARED
WIGGLE	HOPSCOTCH
SHIVER	WINDWARD
TIPTOE	OAF
PIROUETTE	EGG
TWIRL	OBOE
TEETER	NUTMEG
	OBLONG

8

9

WHAT IS FRANGIPANI?

Frangipani is a small flowering tree which grows in tropical places, and beside which people wearing saris and *puggrees* walk.

WHAT IS A PUGGREE?

A *puggree* is a light scarf worn over a hat to protect the *paxwax* from the sun.

WHAT IS THE PAXWAX?

The *paxwax* is the tendon at the back of the neck which supports the head, and which flushes red when people are in a *tirrivee*.

WHAT IS A TIRRIVEE?

A *tirrivee* is a temper. Mothers go into a tirrivee over the *jiggery-pokery* of children.

WHAT IS JIGGERY-POKERY?

Jiggery-pokery is trickery or mischief or hanky-panky on the part of children, such as pretending to be deaf or teasing a *Tantony*.

48   49

Alastair Reid, illustrated by
Ben Shahn
Published by Little, Brown and
Company, Boston, 1958
This copy: 1st edition
260 x 190 mm (10¼ x 7½ in)

Born to Jewish parents in Russia, Shahn arrived in the US at the age of 8, where he was reunited with his father, who had been forced to make his own escape after being persecuted as a revolutionary. The family settled in Brooklyn, and the young Ben trained in lithography and graphic design, as well as studying art at City College and the National Academy of Design. His early training in print work, combined with a left-wing political perspective, meant that he was always clear about his refusal to accept a hierarchical distinction between the 'fine' and applied arts. He was as comfortable with poster design and book illustration as he was with easel painting or creating murals for the Rockefeller Center.

In *Ounce Dice Trice*, Shahn collaborated with the Scottish poet and linguist Alastair Reid to create a book all about the sounds and shapes of words. As the opening text explains, 'All the words here are meant to be said aloud, over and over, for your own delight.' Shahn's illustrations and design perfectly complement – and, at times, dance with – Reid's words to create a form of concrete poetry at around the time that the term was coming into regular use.

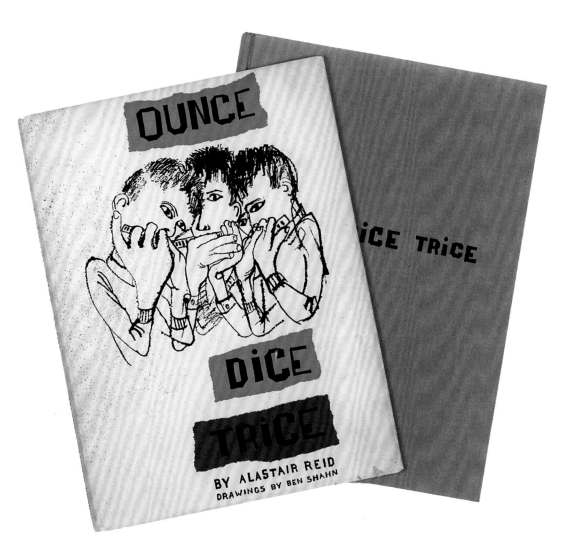

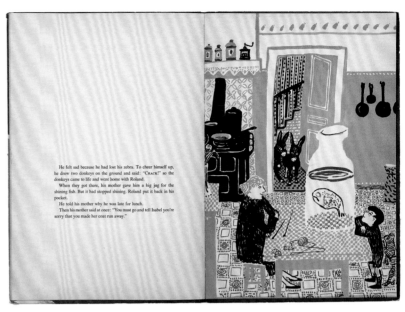

s late to school.

e corner," said the teacher, which Roland did.

was nothing to do in the corner, so with his pencil
a long tiger on the wall. Then he said: "CRACK!" and
e to life.

stretched himself out to his full length and very politely
rning to the teacher.

room for you here," said the teacher, and he opened
bout another word the tiger went away.

y out for recess now," said the teacher. "As for you,
stay in. See to it that you don't say 'CRACK' again."

He felt sad because he had lost his zebra. To cheer himself up,
he drew two donkeys on the ground and said: "CRACK!" so the
donkeys came to life and went home with Roland.

When they got there, his mother gave him a big jug for the
shining fish. But it had stopped shining. Roland put it back in his
pocket.

He told his mother why he was late for lunch.

Then his mother said at once: "You must go and tell Isabel you're
sorry that you made her coat run away."

l, but he

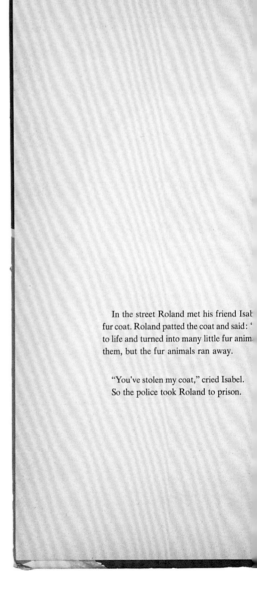

In the street Roland met his friend Isab
fur coat. Roland patted the coat and said: '
to life and turned into many little fur anim
them, but the fur animals ran away.

"You've stolen my coat," cried Isabel.
So the police took Roland to prison.

84

François' hand-rendered titling perfectly complements his freewheeling drawing. Shapes are 'reversed out' and formed by the surrounding colours.

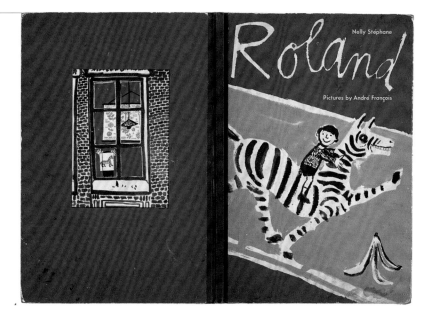

François uses the white of the page as a fourth colour to create this snowy scene.

Nelly Stéphane, illustrated by André François
Published by Harcourt, Brace & Co., New York, 1958
This copy: 1st edition
305 x 210 mm (12 x 8¼ in)

André François was a giant of twentieth-century graphic arts, revered by his peers for his invention, innovation and graphic wit. His output as an artist was divided between theatre design, exhibition and store design, advertising, and editorial and graphic design, as well as book illustration and authorship. He is referred to by the Art Directors Club of New York as 'a graphic arts master whose protean career forms a bridge from the beginnings of modern graphic design to the present'.

François was born in 1915 to a Hungarian Jewish family in Temesvár, in what is now part of Romania. He studied at the Academy of Fine Arts in Budapest, then took French citizenship in 1939. His work has influenced generations of graphic artists, its childlike charm and apparent naivety belying a sophisticated graphic wit.

In Nelly Stéphane's *Roland*, a little boy idly draws animals at school and when he shouts 'Crack!' the animals suddenly become real. François brings the story to life with stunning three-colour separations. Using blue, black and gold, he creates a vibrant pattern and a graphic rhythm. In an interview with Wendy Coates-Smith of the Cambridge School of Art in 2001, François commented on the idea that the childlike quality of his work acted as a 'Trojan horse': 'I think that I'd say that very, very few people are sensitive to art or painting generally speaking. You have to cheat by producing art at the same time as answering the brief. You have to cheat. If you didn't they wouldn't accept your ideas.'

g her
came
catch

Lines can bend like rows of wheat when a soft breeze blows. They can bend in other ways too. Lines that bend in a zigzag way seem to crackle with excitement. They make me think of thunder storms and jagged mountain peaks. I see the huge jaws of a crocodile, wide open and bristling with jagged teeth, ready to snap shut.

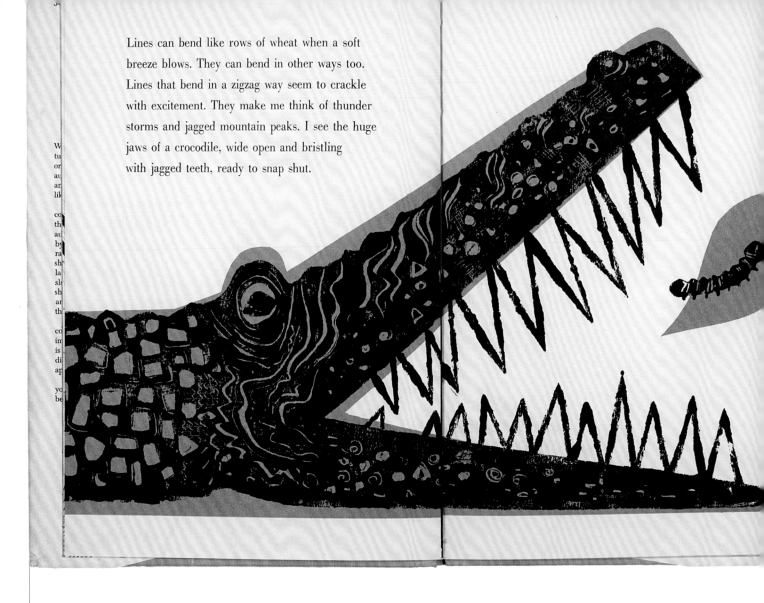

Helen Borten places the irregular, textured black print over a hard-edged, flat blue to great effect.

Simple shapes in primary colours are placed against a black background with occasional overprinting at the edges, making the colours 'dance and sing'.

Slanted lines can rush me downward on a slide or sliding pond. Or they can soar me high on a pair of skis. For slanted lines are like a seesaw—sometimes they go up, and sometimes they come down.

Some colors are as dull as the sky on a rainy day when everything is dripping and gray. Others are so bright they make me blink. Bright colors clang for attention like a fire engine. They are as exciting as city lights flashing on and off after dark.

Borten's pictorial dust jacket covers an elegantly finished binding embossed with a simple red motif.

39
Do You See What I See?

Helen Borten
Published by Abelard-Schuman,
London/New York, 1959
This copy: 1st edition
260 x 182 mm (10¼ x 7¼ in)

After graduating from art school and working extensively as an accomplished designer of book jackets and an illustrator of books with educational themes, this was Borten's first picturebook as sole author. The book, an 'art primer' that elegantly introduces children to the formal qualities of shapes, lines and colours, was one of the *New York Times* top ten picturebooks of 1959. Although its use of limited colour and geometric motifs is redolent of the 1950s, its integration of word and image to explain the power of design was way ahead of its time.

Like many true picturebook makers, Borten has spoken of how working in this field 'resolved an inner conflict' for her – that of wanting to be a painter. She found that the authorial control required to create and realize a complete concept such as this fulfilled her creative needs as an artist.

Borten demonstrates how various visual forms can be employed to create particular effects and evoke special moods. We are introduced to the calming effects of horizontal designs in contrast to soaring verticals. Words are used sparingly but effectively: 'Lines can bend in a curved way, too. A curved line is like a swan, full of beauty and grace. It can rise and curl slowly, as lazy as smoke. It can twirl like a dancer, or flow and swirl like water in a stream full of speckled fish.'

This well-produced hardback book is bound with grey canvas-backed boards, embossed with a red landscape and sun motif, and covered with an illustrated dust jacket.

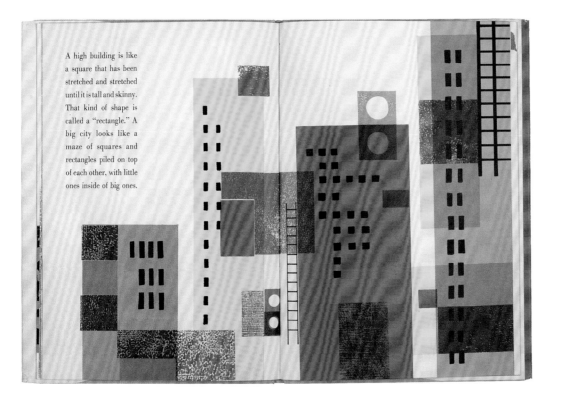

A high building is like a square that has been stretched and stretched until it is tall and skinny. That kind of shape is called a "rectangle." A big city looks like a maze of squares and rectangles piled on top of each other, with little ones inside of big ones.

The children's theatrical gestures create a slow-motion, dreamlike effect.

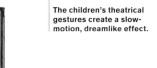

Sendak builds the intense atmosphere of a hot summer's night, using heavily layered brushstrokes of light on dark.

Janice May Udry, illustrated by
Maurice Sendak
Published by Harper & Row,
New York, 1959
This copy: 1st UK edition
(The Bodley Head, 1979)
258 x 185 mm (10¼ x 7¼ in)

Maurice Sendak, who died in
2012, was the Brooklyn-born
son of Jewish-Polish immigrants.
He is perhaps best known for
Where the Wild Things Are, which
was published in 1963 and was
awarded the Caldecott Medal the
following year.

One of Sendak's lesser-
known titles, this is a book that
finds the great master in a lyrical,
sensual mode. Udry's richly
evocative text tells of a sultry,
moonlit summer's night, from the
perspective of a group of children
playing outside before bedtime.
Sendak's images lend an almost
pagan, ritualistic feel to the book
as he uses heavily opaque paint
to create formalized shapes of
trees, buildings and children in
intense moonlight. Using an almost
pointillist technique, the artist
eschews representational interest
in architecture or flora in order to
create a primitive, Rousseau-esque
atmosphere. The children seem to
float and dance across the pages
in an operatic performance, brought
to a close only by summons from
the house:

Mother calls from the door,
'Children, oh children.'
But we're not children, we're the
Moon Jumpers!
'It's time,' she says.

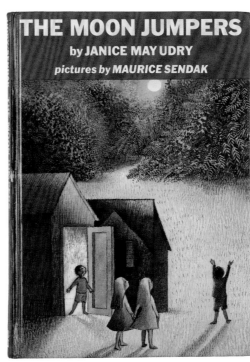

"Wait," said the taxi driver, "that's nothing. You haven't seen the boats in the city." And they drove Petunia to the riverside where boats as big as hills were tied with ropes as big as trees.

They were so big, Petunia felt still smaller.

"Wait," said the policeman, "you haven't seen the deepest street in the city." And they drove Petunia to a street as deep as a crevice in the mountain.

It was so deep, Petunia, at the bottom, felt still smaller.

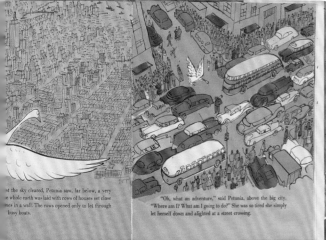

st the sky cleared, Petunia saw, far below, a very
e whole earth was laid with rows of houses set close
nes in a wall. The rows opened only to let through
busy boats.

"Oh, what an adventure," said Petunia, above the big city. "Where am I? What am I going to do?" She was so tired she simply let herself down and alighted at a street crossing.

The next day, the policeman and his wife took Petunia to a railway station so big it would have enclosed a mountain. They kissed Petunia and Petunia waved to them when the train started off.

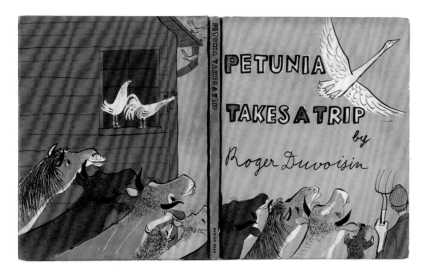

Roger Duvoisin
Published by the Bodley Head,
London, 1959
This copy: 1st edition
260 x 210 mm (10¼ x 8¼ in)

Duvoisin was born in Geneva, Switzerland. He studied at the École Nationale Supérieure des Arts Décoratifs in Paris before going on to work in a number of design fields, including textiles, theatre design and mural painting. He moved to the US with his wife, Louise Fatio, in the 1920s, and became an American citizen in 1938.

Duvoisin's picturebook work led to many awards, including a Caldecott Medal for *White Snow, Bright Snow* (written by Alvin Tresselt). But it was his successful series of animal characters that enjoyed the widest popularity. *The Happy Lion* (1954), written by his wife, was the first of ten books featuring the character; Veronica the hippopotamus was another success. Petunia the goose first appeared in 1950, published by Knopf, and went on to become another long-running favourite.

Duvoisin's simple – sometimes almost crude – line drawing is here supported by flat colour and line-block separations, occasionally using mechanical tints to give texture to the page. The illustrations exude charm and period style as they tell the story of Petunia's journey from the countryside to the big city. Dramatic use of extremes of scale give us Petunia in Penn Station and at the foot of towering skyscrapers in Duvoisin's adopted hometown of New York.

While Petunia ate a triple-decker sandwich the policeman and the taxi driver told her about their city, how beautiful and big it was. "Why," said the policeman, "most houses are bigger than your farmhouse, barns and silo, put together."

"And wait," said the taxi driver, "you wouldn't believe it, even our animals are bigger." And they drove Petunia to a place where trees and grass grew and animals were kept. Indeed, city animals were not at all like those on the farm. Some were so tall—as tall as Maypoles.

And Petunia felt smaller looking up at them . . .

Roger Duvoisin creates texture on the black-and-white spreads by rendering decorative surface patterns.

From her seat by the train window, Petunia watched the green fields, the SMALL houses, the SMALL streams, as they glided by and she felt more and more like a real-size goose again. She was happy.

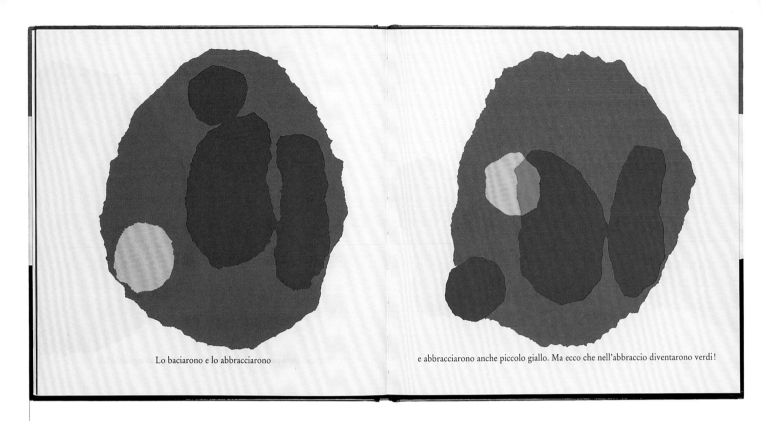

Lo baciarono e lo abbracciarono

e abbracciarono anche piccolo giallo. Ma ecco che nell'abbraccio diventarono verdi!

Lionni chose to use torn rather than cut edges because he felt that a sharp cut would make 'too mechanical a shape for a living thing'.[2]

With minimal material and a complete absence of recognizable characterization, Lionni is still able to bring pace, rhythm and movement to this sequence.

Tutti si abbracciarono con gioia

Piccolo blu e piccolo giallo (Little blue and little yellow)

Leo Lionni
Published by Ivan Obolensky Inc.,
New York, 1959
This copy: 1999 Italian edition
(Babalibri, Milan)
205 x 205 mm (8 x 8 in)

In his autobiography, Lionni recalls the germination of this highly influential picturebook. Taking his 3- and 5-year-old grandchildren on a train journey, packed with other travellers, he realized that he was going to have to think of something clever to prevent misbehaviour:

'I automatically opened my briefcase, took out an advance copy of *Life*, showed the children the cover, and tried to say something funny about the ads as I turned the pages, until a page with a design in blue, yellow and green gave me an idea. "Wait," I said, "I'll tell you a story." I ripped the page out of the magazine and tore it into small pieces. The children followed the proceedings with intense expectancy ... "This is Little Blue and Little Yellow ..."'[1] So was born Lionni's first book for children. He was the first to use collage in children's books in this bold, abstract way.

Lionni was the son of a Sephardic Jew who worked in the diamond industry in the Netherlands. He moved to Philadelphia when he was 14, but later relocated to Italy, where he worked successfully as a painter and designer. In 1939, fleeing the Fascists, he returned to Philadelphia and forged a highly successful career in advertising design, commissioning such leading artists as Saul Steinberg. He later moved to New York, where he worked for Time/Life as the art director of *Fortune* magazine for 14 years. From 1960 he was able to concentrate on his own art and design, including the production of numerous award-winning books.

e i bambini giocarono fino all'ora di cena.

1 *Between Worlds*, by Leo Lionni
   (Alfred A. Knopf, New York, 1997).
2 Ibid.

In the palace yard he saw the horses and brindled hunting hounds lying asleep; on the roof the pigeons sat with their heads tucked under their wings. And as he entered the palace, the flies were sleeping on the walls and the cook in the kitchen was still stretching out his hand to catch the boy. He went on and saw the whole court lying asleep in the hall, and the King and Queen up by the throne. He went still further and everything was so quiet that he could hear his own breathing. At last he came to the tower and opened the door of the little room where Briar Rose was sleeping.

The old man had heard from his grandfather that many kings' sons had already tried to force their way through the hedge of thorns, but had stuck fast and died a sorry death. Then the young man said: "I am not afraid. I will go and see the beautiful Briar Rose." The good old man tried to dissuade him, but he would not listen.

The hundred years had now passed by and the day had come for Briar Rose to wake again. When the King's son reached the hedge of thorns it turned into a mass of large and beautiful flowers which parted to let him pass unharmed, closing up into a hedge again behind him.

43
The Sleeping Beauty

Felix Hoffmann
Published by H. R. Sauerländer & Co., Aarau, Switzerland, 1959
This copy: 1st UK edition (Oxford University Press, London/ Oxford, 1959)
300 x 215 mm (12 x 8½ in)

Hoffmann was an artist who specialized in the fairly tale – in particular, the works of the Brothers Grimm – and was not restricted to the book as his stage. He was a master glass engraver, mural painter and printmaker whose respect for this particular area of literature is evident across the various forms of his creative output. He can be seen as belonging to a Swiss tradition of internationally celebrated graphic artists that includes Hans Fischer and Celestino Piatti. Hoffmann enjoyed particular popularity in Japan, where his books have sold in their hundreds of thousands. He died in 1975 at the age of 64.

The highly respected Swiss children's literature critic Bettina Hürliman wrote of his work in relation to his fellow countrymen: 'Felix Hoffman is assuredly the most versatile of these artists … it is his fairy stories in particular which exemplify his unparalleled ability to combine perfect craftsmanship with the delight of story-telling.'[1]

For *The Sleeping Beauty*, Hoffmann worked directly on the lithographic plate, bringing his printmaking experience to the final printed book. The book is printed on a rather course cartridge paper, heightening the sense of viewing and holding original prints as the pages are turned. The artist's visual language is characteristically classical and theatrical throughout.

1 *Picture-Book World*, by Bettina Hürlimann, (Oxford University Press, London, 1968).

Tunnicliffe combined depth
and atmosphere with clarity
of information.

When we see the hazel catkins turn yellow, we know that spring is not far off. The catkins, sometimes called lambs' tails, are a drooping string of small flowerets that bear only stamens. Each flower produces a large number of pollen grains. These are wafted on the wind, and a few fall on the stigmas of the scarlet female flowers, which are too small to show in this picture. From the meeting of the male and female flowers, nuts grow slowly to ripen in September. At the base of the nut-sapling, honeysuckle vines are putting out their first, tender green leaves, another sign that spring is coming.

The blackbird has his springtime plumage, and very smart indeed he looks. His wife, who is away building her nest, is brownish, and does not have a yellow bill. The rooks in the elm-tops are beginning to show an interest in their last year's nests, which they will soon be rebuilding. The elm blossoms are beginning to show a purple tint, and will be even brighter coloured by early spring.

On the pasture a flock of green and golden plovers has settled. The green plovers have crested heads, and remain with us all through the year; but the golden plovers take long voyages to far distant lands. Two swans are swimming on the lake.

40

fine weather
cks towards
ke. Already
most of the
le swoop to
e flocks are
more birds
rings can be
ng of their
k loudly in

t wonderful
us to linger
omes colder.

night, since
aces among

and early
or eight to-
more. On
n, who goes
he can find
aying wood.

The Ladybird format of full-
colour dust jacket over single-
colour, paper-covered boards
is simple and elegant.

E. L. Grant Watson, illustrated by
C. F. Tunnicliffe
Published by Ladybird Books,
Loughborough, 1959
This copy: 1st edition
180 x 115 mm (7 x 4½ in)

Children growing up in the 1950s and 1960s would have found it difficult to avoid Ladybird Books. The winning formula of pocket-sized hardbacks depicting stereotypical white middle-class family life meant that the huge range of titles was found in abundance on every British high street. The name of the publishing company behind the books was in fact Wills & Hepworth, but its Ladybird imprint became so universally recognized that in 1971 it began trading as Ladybird Books.

Many of the books featured illustrations that were photographically posed and skilfully painted in gouache by such regular artists as Harry Wingfield and Martin Aitchison. C. F. (Charles Frederick) Tunnicliffe was, along with S. R. Badmin (see page 45), the 'go to' artist for representational illustrations of the British countryside and its flora and fauna. Tunnicliffe's work was familiar to millions through his illustrations for numerous series of the cards included in packs of Brooke Bond tea.

The four Ladybird 'What to Look for' books cover each of the seasons. Tunnicliffe and Grant Watson collaborated on many books about the British countryside, Tunnicliffe often working in his most favoured black-and-white medium, scraperboard (or scratchboard). Here, the artist is given a full-colour page on every spread, and his paintings reflect his deep knowledge both of the countryside and the subtle colours and tones of midwinter. Tunnicliffe balances superbly his painterly instincts with the need for illustrative clarity.

Her **FATHER** was a fisherman. Every day he went out in his boat to tend his fish traps.

Her **MOTHER** was busy doing the work in ➡

6

7

Maria closed her eyes, and when she opened them what in the wide world do you suppose she saw standing there on the beach, very large and very gentle?

33

34

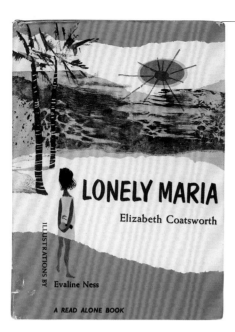

45
Lonely Maria

Elizabeth Coatsworth, illustrated by Evaline Ness
Published by Pantheon Books, New York, 1960
This copy: 1st UK edition (Hamish Hamilton, 1967)
213 x 157 mm (8½ x 6½ in)

Ness was one of the giants of American illustration. After being a runner-up for the Caldecott Medal for three successive years, she was awarded it in 1967 for perhaps her best-known book, *Sam, Bangs, and Moonshine*. Ness (who retained her surname from her second marriage, to the legendary FBI investigator Eliot Ness) worked for some time as a fashion illustrator in New York before working on children's books.

Lonely Maria was a collaboration with Elizabeth Coatsworth, and is set on an island in the West Indies. The island is as much the lead character as is Maria, a young girl who is the only child of her age on the island. The images and text present a rich, sensual sense of place as they describe the food, flora, smells and general atmosphere of lazy tropical-island life. Created as four-colour woodcut separations, the images are elegant and stylish (reflecting the artist's fashion-drawing training), yet at the same time raw and expressive.

Perhaps the elephant wasn't quite like other elephants. Maria had seen a picture of an elephant named Jumbo in her mother's old geography book, but she hadn't looked at it carefully.

Still, he was very large and grand. And he *was* an elephant. From the moment she laid eyes on him, Maria loved him.

She named him **JUMBO**

35

Daring, sweeping
brushstrokes lend an
almost calligraphic
feel to the page.

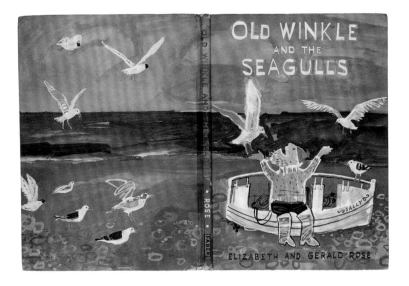

The stylized, almost
cartoonish depiction
of figures seems to
sit comfortably with a
more representational
approach to landscape.

Suddenly he saw a teeming mass of gulls wheeling
and screaming, turning and whirling, above a shoal of fish.

Elizabeth Rose, illustrated by
Gerald Rose
Published by Faber & Faber,
London, 1960
This copy: 1st edition
250 x 185 mm (10 x 7¼ in)

Winner of the Kate Greenaway
Medal for 1960, this book placed
Gerald Rose firmly on the map as a
book illustrator while he was still in
his mid-twenties. He has continued
to illustrate prolifically ever since,
as well as working for many years
as an educator, having been in
charge of illustration at Maidstone
College of Art in the UK in the
1970s and 1980s.

Rose was born in Hong Kong,
and as a child during World War II
he experienced the trauma of his
family's detention by the occupying
Japanese forces. Later, in England,
he studied at Lowestoft School of
Art and London's Royal Academy.
Many of his early picturebooks,
including this one, were created
in collaboration with his wife,
Elizabeth. However, he went on to
work with many other writers, as
well as reworking and interpreting
traditional tales from a range
of cultures. Rose took particular
delight in representing animal
characters, depicting them in
vibrant colours.

Old Winkle and the Seagulls
is an enduring classic. Composed
of alternating colour and black-
and-white spreads, the artwork
is rendered with vibrant, airy
brushwork that brilliantly evokes
its nautical theme, underpinned
by a dynamic design and the use
of pattern and texture in areas
of colour.

**This spectacular double-page
spread was informed by direct
observation of gulls in flight
and the many, varied shapes
that they make.**

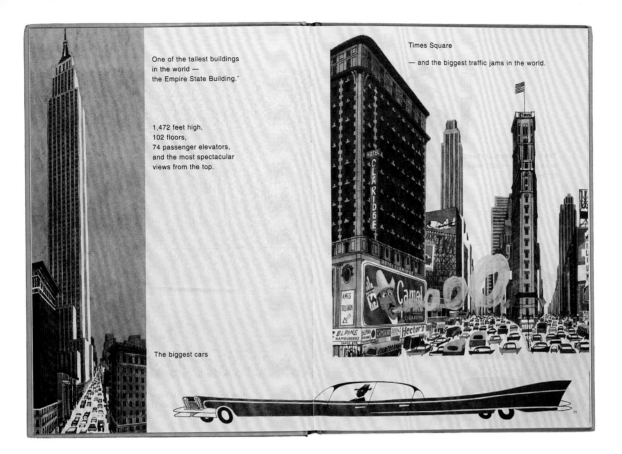

One of the tallest buildings
in the world —
the Empire State Building.*

1,472 feet high,
102 floors,
74 passenger elevators,
and the most spectacular
views from the top.

Times Square

— and the biggest traffic jams in the world.

The biggest cars

11

The scale and drama of the
sports stadium is set against
a single football player in
full regalia.

Everything in A
wonderfully wr

Yankee Stadium

Baseball or football fans — 70,000 strong —
come here to watch their heroes.*

— including fo

56

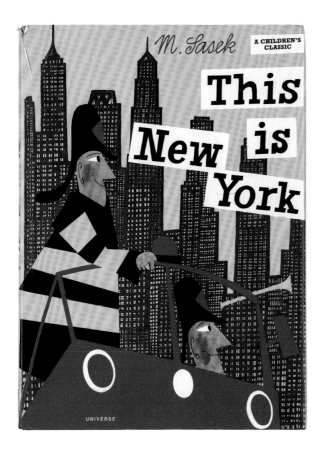

Miroslav Sasek
Published by Macmillan,
London, 1960
This copy: 2003 US edition
(Universe Publishing, New York)
320 x 230 mm (12½ x 9 in)

Miroslav (or 'M.', as he always
signed his work) Sasek's 'This Is'
series ran from 1959, when *This
is Paris* appeared, through to *This
is Historic Britain* in 1974. Each
book introduces the reader to a city
or country.

Perhaps the key to the success
of this iconic and influential
series is the childlike sense of
wonder that pervades each of
the books – 'drawn' in both words
and pictures. Much more than
standard non-fiction guides full of
monuments and landmarks, Sasek
was able to create books full of
humour and anecdotal detail that
captured the feel of the everyday
life and culture of each destination.
Often visiting these places for the
first time himself, he would spend
several weeks there, working solidly
on a book while immersed in the
local culture.

Sasek was born and brought
up in Czechoslovakia, where he
studied art and architecture before
leaving when the Communists
came to power in 1948. The
first book of the series was
conceived during a trip to Paris,
where he observed the apparent
failure of other visiting parents
to engage their children with their
surroundings. *This is New York*
is one of the earliest in the series
and shows Sasek at his very
best. (There is a freshness and
expressive graphic vitality about
the early books that became less
apparent as the series grew in
popularity.) The life of New York
City is captured at every level with
the incisive insight of the émigré.

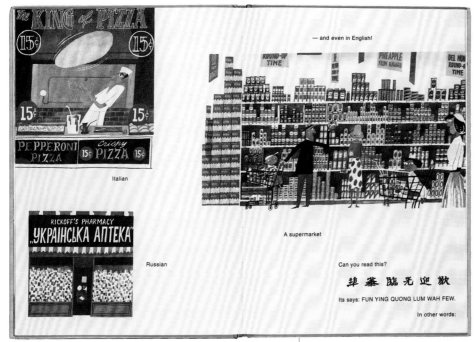

**Sasek's reporter's eye
spans everyday anecdotal
details as well as universally
known landmarks.**

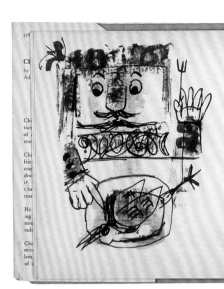

When Corrado saw that one leg was missing from the crane, he could not believe his eyes. In a loud voice he called Chichibio from the kitchen and asked him where the other leg was.

"Sir, cranes have only one leg," said Chichibio, who was a big liar. "If you don't believe me, go see for yourself."

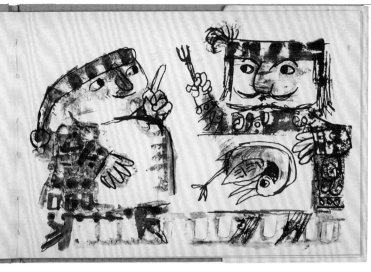

All the guests at the table burst out laughing. But Corrado did not laugh. He frowned and said, "Very well, Chichibio.

Tomorrow we shall go look at a few live cranes. And if it turns out that you have told me a lie, I shall punish you."

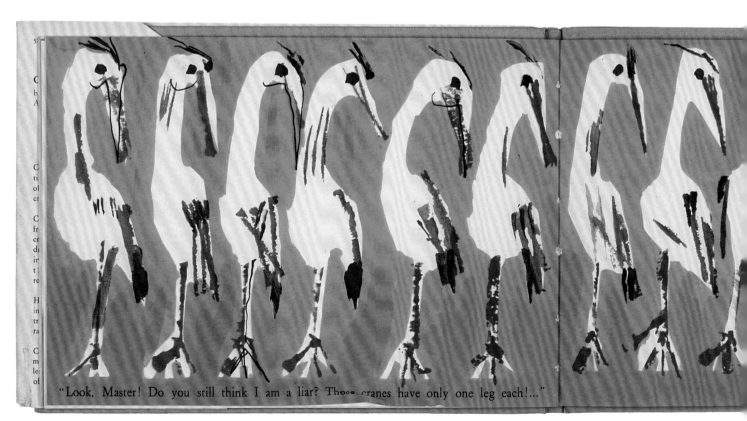

"Look, Master! Do you still think I am a liar? These cranes have only one leg each!..."

Line and wash illustrations on the single-colour pages are perfectly weighted to balance with the text.

Giovanni Boccaccio, adapted and illustrated by Emanuele Luzzati
Published by Ivan Obolensky Inc., New York, 1961
This copy: 1st edition
175 x 245 mm (7 x 9½ in)

Emanuele (Lele) Luzzati died in 2007 at the age of 85 after a long and productive career as a stage and costume designer, film-maker, ceramicist and book illustrator. His collaborations with Giulio Gianini led to Oscar-nominated short animations set to opera overtures by Rossini. Luzzati also designed widely for opera, including *The Magic Flute* at Glyndebourne in 1963. Mozart's opera held a particular fascination for him, and many years later he created a Magic Flute park for children at a seaside resort in Liguria. Revered in Italy for his wide-ranging graphic output, there is now a magnificent museum devoted to his work; the Museo Luzzati is housed in one of the ancient stone gates to the city of Genova.

Chichibio and the Crane was Luzzati's first book for children. Boccaccio's tale tells of a grand nobleman who shoots a crane and gives it to his cook, Chichibio, to prepare for dinner. As he pulls the bird from the oven, Chichibio is persuaded to give one of the legs to the beautiful Brunetta, whose attentions he desires. The book charmingly follows his subsequent attempts to evade his master's wrath by persuading him that all cranes have only one leg.

The spreads are printed on alternate page spreads as four-colour half-tone separations and single-colour half-tones. Luzzati's bold, expressive mark making is always underpinned by a consummate sense of design.

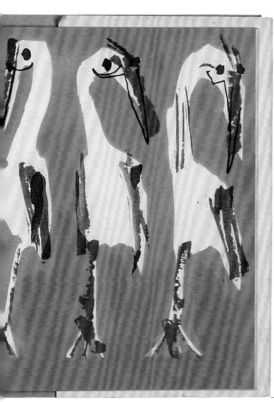

Limited to four colours, Luzzati uses expressive sweeps of wash and crudely cut relief print to create and define dynamic shapes.

He heard the birds singing.

All at once the General came upon a field of beautiful flowers. Never had he seen such a wonderful sight. There were more kinds of flowers than he had ever imagined, and more colours than any artist had ever dreamed of.

General Jodpur stood quite still for a few minutes, and then he slowly walked across the field and sat down in the middle of the flowers. He watched the bees buzzing in and out, searching for pollen to make honey. He thought that one would be sure to land on his nose, but the bees were far too busy to notice even a famous general.

Foreman's highly stylized use of pattern predates the 'flower power' era by several years.

e farmers started to plough their fields and sow seeds for the next harvest.

Elegant use of white space
is a strong feature of the
book's design.

49
The General

Janet Charters, illustrated by
Michael Foreman
Published by Routledge &
Kegan Paul, London, 1961
This copy: 1st edition
270 x 210 mm (10½ x 8¼ in)

Although Foreman has enjoyed a
long and highly successful career
in book illustration, this early
picturebook is one of his finest
achievements. The result of a
husband-and-wife collaboration,
the book is a very early precursor
of the 'flower power' mood of a
few years later, telling the story of
a much-decorated army general
who falls from his horse in a forest
and undergoes a transformative
experience involving nature,
peace and love. Foreman's richly
decorative, graphic use of paint and
space is stylistically different from
his later, more familiar work with
transparent layers of wash. The use
of gouache and inks is typical of
the period, but Foreman's dynamic
use of white space is particularly
impressive, delivering the book's
anti-war message with great style.

Foreman was born in Suffolk
and studied at the local Lowestoft
School of Art; he later attended
the Royal College of Art in London,
where he won a silver medal and
a travel scholarship to the US.
Foreman went on to work as an art
director, both in the US (*Playboy*
magazine) and the UK, and to teach
at art schools in the UK, including
Saint Martin's School of Art and the
Central School of Art and Design
(prior to the merging of the two)
and the Royal College of Art.

General Jodpur was not hurt. He landed on soft grass. The
grass was so soft and smelled so sweet that, to his surprise, the
General found that he did not want to move. He picked a piece
of grass, put it between his teeth, and lay back in the warm
sunshine.

After a long time he decided that he
ought to be getting back to camp.
Reluctantly he got to his feet and
set off at a brisk march.
Although he had ridden along the
path many times, he now noticed
things he had never seen before
because he was always going so fast.
He saw squirrels and rabbits and field
mice and hedge hogs and swallows
and wood pigeons, and even a
peacock.

Adolphus William went slowly across the lawn, under the flowers, beneath the bushes, and around the fruit trees, when – Tom, Dick, and Harry Starling saw him. They divided him neatly into three equal parts. 'That was good', said Tom. 'Wasn't it sweet', said Dick. 'I like 'em tender', said Harry. And then quite suddenly Tom, Dick, and Harry, were sick.

James Gustavus Adolphus William wriggled home in three little bits. Mummie *was* surprised! James Gus, tavus Adolph, us William, were bandaged and put to bed. 'Little worms', said Mrs Busy Bee to her daughter Zipporah, who had seen what had happened, 'can't smell because they haven't a nose. Little worms can't see because they haven't eyes. Little worms should do what their mummie tells them to do.' 'Yes, Mummie', said Zipporah, as she flew away to the Forget-me-Nots like a good girl.

TAKE THE BROOM

THE STORY OF ANT ANN

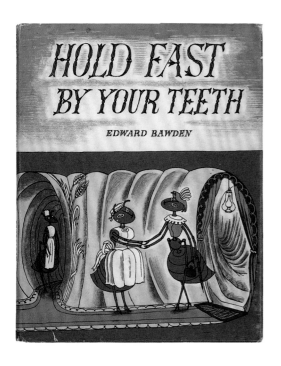

HOLD FAST BY YOUR TEETH

EDWARD BAWDEN

On the train is an Infantile Marine. 'Mate, pipe down at Shrimpton-on-Sea', he cries. 'Sure!' cried Richard.

(His hat is Marks & Spencer)

50
Hold Fast by Your Teeth

Edward Bawden
Published by Routledge &
Kegan Paul, London, 1963
This copy: 1st edition
270 x 210 mm (10½ x 8¼ in)

It has to be said that Edward Bawden was not a natural illustrator for children. As the dust jacket blurb observes, this collection of stories is 'amusing and heartless, and such as any good father would like to be able to tell and sketch if he had the ability'. The book is in the form of an elaboration upon a collection of tales that Bawden had told to his children. They are perverse and indeed rather heartless. Bawden was one of the greatest of British graphic artists, but he did not 'do' warmth. Nevertheless, the book as a whole is a fascinating period piece, full of the author's wry, detached and, at times, puerile humour, both visual and verbal. It is populated by an unusual array of characters, both animal and human, and there are moments of the kind of casual racism that would be unthinkable today.

It is the sheer brilliance of Bawden's designs and the production quality of the book (printed at the legendary W. S. Cowell of Ipswich) that make this such an attractive addition to his vast overall output. Printed in black line with rich, flat-colour separations on relatively coarse paper, each page feels like an original print. Bawden's son, Richard, who features prominently in the stories, is now a highly regarded artist-printmaker in his own right. Copies of the book, which was in only one edition, are now relatively scarce and expensive.

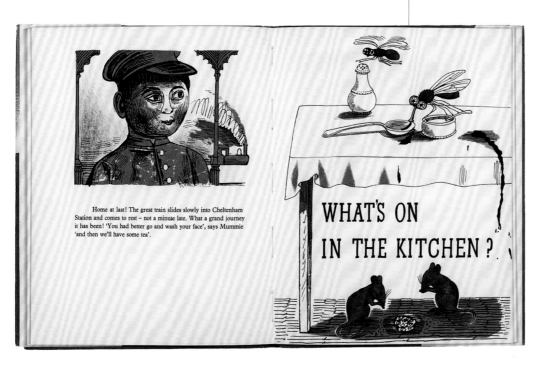

Home at last! The great train slides slowly into Cheltenham Station and comes to rest – not a minute late. What a grand journey it has been! 'You had better go and wash your face', says Mummie 'and then we'll have some tea'.

WHAT'S ON
IN THE KITCHEN ?

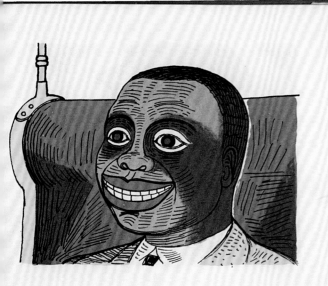

Black line and colour separations exploit Bawden's consummate printmaking skills in an image that would be seen as offensive today but was typical of the casual racism of the time.

On the train is Prince Chungagunga. He says, 'Shuck-u-out, poppa pop pop, shuck a shu, poppa de pop, Stratford on Avon for de Bard.' 'Chuck you out, I will', says Richard. 'You look like a Prince but you talk like a child.'

(The Prince wears no hat)

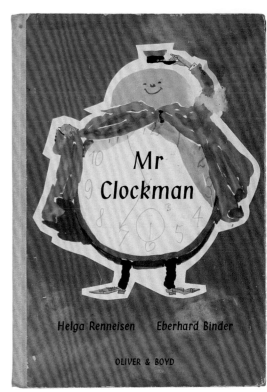

Mr
Clockman

Helga Renneisen   Eberhard Binder

OLIVER & BOYD

"Tock krrr, tock krrr, tock krrr," creaked the old town
hall clock. Her hands moved slowly, and her voice rasped
when she spoke.

"Well, krrr krrr, if it isn't a little alarm clock!"
she wheezed. "What are you doing up here, little man?"

"Do you know, by any chance, when small children have
to go to sleep?" chimed the little clockman.

"I couldn't tell you," rasped the town hall clock.
"I don't have anything to do with little children. But
I do know when the town councillors come to work in the
morning. And I also know that they often work until it
is very late. But when small children have to go to bed,
that I couldn't say." The voice of the old clock rolled
and rattled. "Krrr krrr. I can't see any children in
the streets. They must all have gone to sleep."

"No, they haven't," Dora butted in. "They are playing
at home—or in the garden. You can't see them, that's
all."

"Perhaps that's it," croaked the old clock. "You may
be right. Krrr krrr."

The little clockman looked at Dora. Then he said,
"Thank you, Aunt, and good night."

51
Mr Clockman

Helga Renneisen, illustrated by
Eberhard Binder
Published as *Vom Dorle,
das nicht schlafen wollte* by
Kinderbuchverlag, Berlin, 1964
This copy: 1st UK edition
(Oliver & Boyd, Edinburgh, 1967)
275 x 190 mm (10¾ x 7½ in)

This is a rare example of a German picturebook appearing in English in the 1960s; it had first appeared in Germany as *Vom Dorle, das nicht schlafen wollte* (About Dorle, Who Did Not Want to Go to Sleep). *Mr Clockman* is, for modern readers, a somewhat less than 'correct' bedtime tale of a mother and father going out to the cinema for the evening and leaving their daughter at home to cry herself to sleep. The ensuing adventure, however, makes it all worthwhile. Mr Clockman takes little Dora (Dorle) from her high-rise apartment and off on a night-time flight over the lights of the city, from clock to clock in search of an answer to the question, 'What time do little children have to be asleep?' It is Binder's fabulous use of colour and scale that brings this journey to life. His expressive, watery brushstrokes seem to have been applied with minimal preparation and maximum gesture, some of the rough pencil lines still being visible through the vibrant colour.

Binder grew up in Magdeburg and, during World War II, studied commercial art in Hildesheim. He graduated in 1952 from Magdeburg's School of Applied Arts, in what was by then the German Democratic Republic. He then began a career as a commercial artist and book illustrator, gradually building a reputation with illustrations for such classics as *Tom Sawyer*, *Gulliver's Travels* and *Moby Dick*.

Binder's daughter, Christiane, is an academic at the University of Dortmund, specializing in children's literature; his son Thomas is a book illustrator.

Now Dora could see into the factory yard. The doors of the enormous great sheds stood wide open. Dora knew they made tram rails here.

The glider sank lower and lower, until it landed right next to the factory clock over the entrance. The factory clock was watching the workers passing through the big gate.

"Good evening," said the little clockman politely.

The factory clock looked at the little clockman in surprise. "What do you want, titch?" it said. "Not after work, by any chance? We don't take on people as small as you." It gave a little chuckle.

"No, no," said the clockman. "We only want to ask you what time little girls should be in bed."

The factory clock rattled, and narrowed its eyes. Then it said, "Aren't you Dora? Shouldn't you have been asleep long ago?"

But Dora said loudly, "Of course not. I can always stay up as late as I like."

"Well, I don't know everything, after all," said the factory clock. "Perhaps the school clock can help you."

"You're quite right!" said the clockman. "We should have asked the school clock at the start. Many thanks."

Burningham's use of gouache and wax-resist crayon gives his portrayal of London streets a gritty, atmospheric texture.

They lived in a small street where Humbert had a stable on the ground floor and Mr Firkin had the rooms above.

Every day Humbert and Mr Firkin set out early to start collecting the scrap. Mr Firkin used to keep to the quieter streets as much as possible so as not to meet too much traffic which Humbert did not like.

Humbert had a friend who lived a few doors down. He was a horse that pulled a cart full of flowers and shrubs, and whenever Humbert had a chance he would take a bite as his friend pulled the cart past the stable door.

Mr Firkin and Humbert travelled through dockland sometimes. Humbert liked the smells of food there.

One of the rear wheels of the coach had broken. The coach toppled down and the horses came to a stop. There was a hush. Everyone was aghast.

Such a thing had never occurred in all the hundreds of years since the Show began.

Then lots of things happened all at once.

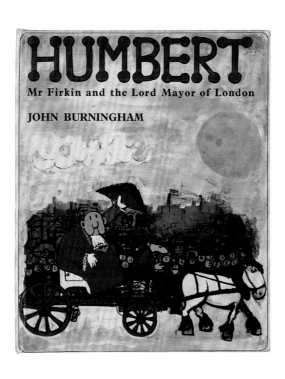

HUMBERT
Mr Firkin and the Lord Mayor of London
JOHN BURNINGHAM

A natural sense of design and composition flows through every double-page spread, typified here by the use of strong shapes and areas of white.

John Burningham
Published by Jonathan Cape,
London, 1965
This copy: 1st edition
265 x 215 mm (10½ x 8½ in)

One of the greatest picturebook innovators of his generation, Burningham has consistently pushed at the boundaries of the medium with such works as *Granpa* and *Come Away from the Water Shirley*. His precocious, Kate Greenaway Medal-winning debut, *Borka: The Adventures of a Goose with No Feathers*, was published in 1963. This was just over three years after he had received his diploma from the Central School of Art in London, giving notice of a unique talent that was emerging at a key time for illustration and, in particular, the picturebook. The development of new methods of lithographic printing, and the vision of such important figures in UK publishing as Tom Maschler at Jonathan Cape and Mabel George at Oxford University Press, helped initiate a 'great leap forward' in expressive picturebook art.

Humbert was Burningham's fourth picturebook from his early post-art-school years. The book tells of a humble working horse in London whose owner trundles him daily through the city, collecting scrap on his cart. One day, the Lord Mayor's parade passes by and Humbert leaps into action to save the day when the Mayor's grand coach breaks down. More than anything, though, the book is a visual celebration of London, a tour through the deep browns of dirty Victorian buildings and the heavy, smog-laden nights, lit by a yellow moon.

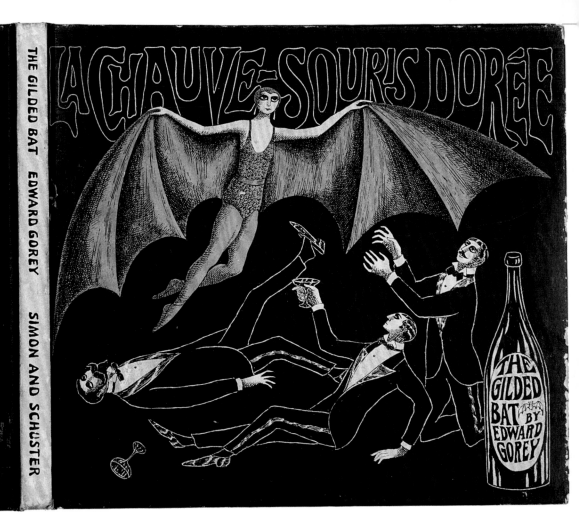

nt anything.

Gorey's extensive knowledge
of ballet is condensed into an
absurdist sequence of moments
from a dancer's career.

A simple text–image arrangement
gives prominence to Gorey's
intense comic tableaux.

53

La chauve-souris dorée
(The gilded bat)

Edward Gorey
Published by Simon & Schuster,
New York, 1966
This copy: 1st edition
160 x 180 mm (6¼ x 7 in)

The word 'unique' tends to be
much overused, but in the context
of the magnificent Edward Gorey
it is essential and appropriate.
Gorey's world of pseudo English
Victorian/Edwardian silliness is
populated by an impressive array
of sinister ne'er-do-wells, unwitting
victims, unexpected guests (human
and indeterminate), inanimate
objects that hover alarmingly, and
much more besides. All of this is
expressed through painstakingly
detailed rendering in pen and ink,
which heightens the tableau effect
of the drawings.

Gorey was an extremely erudite,
cultured man who lived life mostly
alone at his home (Elephant House,
now the Edward Gorey House)
on Cape Cod, emerging religiously
to attend performances of the New
York City Ballet, but also in later
years opening the doors of his
home to stage elaborate theatrical
performances for friends.

Born in Chicago, Gorey
attended art school only briefly –
one semester at the School of the
Art Institute of Chicago, which he
described as 'negligible' in terms
of its influence on his work. He
went on to study French at Harvard.
Gorey's early career was spent
as an employee of the publishing
house Doubleday, where he worked
in the art department and gained
experience illustrating a range of
book covers. After the publication
of his first self-authored work, *The
Unstrung Harp*, in 1953, Gorey's
career as an author took off. *The
Gilded Bat* had originally appeared
serially in *Ballet Review*, and (if it
is possible to summarize a Gorey
'plot') follows the somewhat
overwrought ups and downs of
a ballet career.

Maud obtained a place in the corps of the Ballet Hochepot.

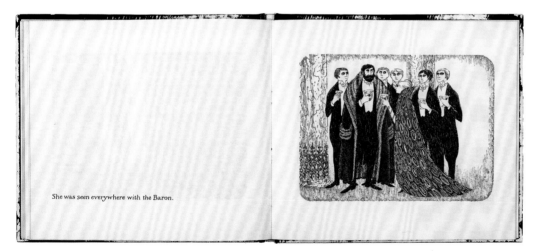

She was seen everywhere with the Baron.

Carefully considered
compositions allow the text
to be integrated naturally
into the page designs.

FROM A RAILWAY CARRIAGE

Faster than fairies, faster than witches,
Bridges and houses, hedges and ditches;
And charging along like troops in a battle,
All through the meadows the horses and cattle:
All of the sights of the hill and the plain
Fly as thick as driving rain;
And ever again, in the wink of an eye,
Painted stations whistle by.

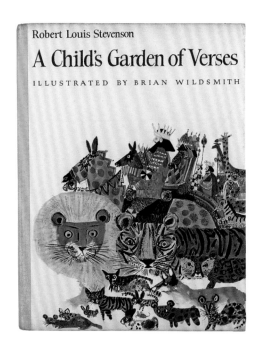

'The Land of Counterpane'
is perhaps the most famous
poem in the collection.
Despite his use of vibrant
colours, Wildsmith manages
to capture the melancholy
tone of the text.

Here is a child who clambers and scrambles,
All by himself and gathering brambles;
Here is a tramp who stands and gazes;
And there is the green for stringing the daisies!
Here is a cart run away in the road
Lumping along with man and load;
And here is a mill and there is a river:
Each a glimpse and gone for ever!

54
A Child's Garden of Verses

Robert Louis Stevenson,
illustrated by Brian Wildsmith
Published by Oxford University
Press, Oxford, 1966
This copy: 1st edition
282 x 220 mm (11 x 8¾ in)

Stevenson's iconic collection
has inspired countless artists
since it first appeared in 1885
under the title *Penny Whistles*.
Brian Wildsmith's lavishly illustrated
version emerged from his long-
standing partnership with Oxford
University Press and, in particular,
the editor Mabel George, who
championed his work and sought
out printers who could do justice
to such a vibrant, painterly world.
It was the company Graphischer
Großbetrieb in Austria that was
entrusted with the task.

Brian Wildsmith grew up
in Yorkshire and, after studying
at Barnsley School of Art, was
awarded a scholarship to the
Slade in London, where he studied
under the influential painter and
administrator William Coldstream.
Despite his strong love of Yorkshire,
Wildsmith's yearning for sunlight
has led him to live in southern
France, where he pursues his first
love, painting. But his picturebooks
are as popular as ever, in all parts
of the world, with many still in print.
He enjoys particular acclaim in
Japan, where the Brian Wildsmith
Museum of Art is devoted to his
work. The museum building was
built as a replica of his family home
and studio in Castellas, France.

Wildsmith's illustrations for
Stevenson's much-loved poems
may be regarded by some as too
dominant, the sheer exuberance
of his colours and brushstrokes
seeming at times to come close
to sweeping the text from the page.
But this is Wildsmith at his most
graphically assured.

He came upon a garden party
where people in gorgeous
costumes were dancing.
"Look! Someone has come as
the man in the moon," a lady
cried. The Moon Man danced
blissfully for hours.

Alas, a grumpy killjoy complained of the late music
to the police. Scared by the sight of the guns and uniforms,

the Moon Man dashed off to the nearby woods.
But he was spotted by the policemen, and a wild chase began.

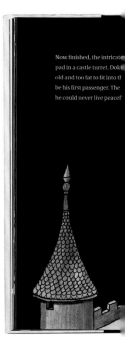

Now finished, the intricat
pad in a castle turret. Dok
old and too fat to fit into t
be his first passenger. The
he could never live peacef

The white moon motif appears throughout the book, and is here used to accommodate text.

55
Moon Man

Tomi Ungerer
Published by Diogenes Verlag, Zurich, 1966
This copy: 2009 English edition
(Phaidon, London)
310 x 240 mm (12¼ x 9½ in)

After Ungerer failed his high-school leaving exams, his school report described him as a 'willfully perverse and subversive individualist'. These qualities have stood him in good stead in a career in graphic commentary, which has so far spanned six decades and covered architectural design, advertising design, sculpture, political posters (against racism, fascism, war and environmental damage) and children's books. He has worked all over the world and been awarded numerous honours, including the Légion d'Honneur in France. In 2007 the Tomi Ungerer Museum opened in his native Strasbourg, and has since been voted one of Europe's ten best museums by the Council of Europe.

First published in Germany as *Der Mondmann*, *Moon Man*, which was made into an animated film by Stephan Schesch in 2012, tells the story of the Man on the Moon's urge to visit the Earth. When he achieves his aim, he is immediately locked up as an alien. His escape, his encounters with the good and the bad to be found on Earth, and his eventual return home are described with sensitivity, humour and that all-important subversive individualism.

Ungerer's unmistakable line wobbles with curiosity as it explores the vicissitudes of life among the inhabitants of the planet that the eponymous hero has observed from afar.

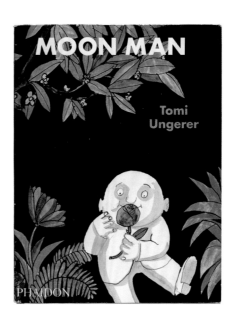

Text is reversed out of solid black, allowing translations for foreign language co-editions to be 'pasted in' without reprinting all four colours.

selling ice-cream. Jules had a chocolate one with a strawberry centre. Fenella spent a long time choosing three flavours for her cornet: in the end she settled on raspberry, 'mocha' or coffee, and 'praline' which had a delicious taste of almonds. They licked them as they set off again down the sandy track which led to their hotel.

Fenella and Jules had a rest in the village square, in the cool green shade of the great plane trees. Some men were playing boule, rolling big metal balls along the dusty ground. It looked a quiet enough game, but they all grew terribly excited over it. At one end of the square sat a lady

Just beyond the last bamboo screen lay the beach. There were lots of people, swimming or floating, diving or sploshing, or else just lying about waiting to turn brown. Fenella had just learnt how to swim, and had never seen such clear water. Jules lent her his diving-mask. "I saw hundreds of tiny fish by the rocks, and they came and tickled my feet!" she said.

David Gentleman
Published by Jonathan Cape,
London, 1967
This copy: 1st edition
150 x 150 mm (6 x 6 in)

Gentleman's long career as an artist and designer has embraced editorial illustration, postage stamps, posters and mural designs for a London Underground station. His work in book illustration has also been prolific, this series of four little hardback picturebooks being one of the highlights. The unusually small scale of the books gives them a jewel-like quality. The series uses the character of Fenella to introduce children to the culture of the featured countries. In *Artwork*, Gentleman says of the series: 'These four books, my first for children, were about the things my small daughter Fenella liked to do, see and eat on holiday in Greece, Ireland, Spain or the South of France. The pictures – in watercolour, with no pen line – were held together by only the slightest of stories. The idea had begun with a little booklet of sketches that I'd once sent home to the real Fenella, when I was away painting in Greece, to show her what the place was like; but Ireland and France were sparked off by real holidays we'd had together.'[1]

Showing 'what the place was like' has been a key concern of Gentleman's throughout his illustrious career as one of the foremost graphic artists of his generation.

The path twisted up very steeply; even after it had gone through an archway into the village it still went winding up and up like a narrow staircase. But it was cooler in the shady streets, and the fresh sound of water came from a fountain. In one of the dark archways, men were blowing glass. They heated it in a furnace until it was white-hot and as soft as syrup; then each man lifted a blob of it out on the end of a hollow pipe, and blew it up like a soap bubble. As it cooled, they rolled it into shape: a bottle or a jar, or perhaps a bowl. Fenella watched them making some tiny jugs and glasses, and she bought one of each.

1   *Artwork*, by David Gentleman (Ebury Press, London, 2002).

Traditional perspective is largely ignored in favour of pure design. Line is created through the scraping away of a layer of paint to reveal the colour beneath.

Piatti rarely missed an opportunity to include in his work his favourite motif, the owl.

57
Zirkus Nock (The Nock Family Circus)

Celestino Piatti
Published by Artemis Verlag,
Zurich and Stuttgart, 1967
This copy: 1st edition
215 x 300 mm (8½ x 11¾ in)

The Swiss graphic artist Celestino Piatti trained at what is today known as the Zurich University of Applied Sciences, and was a prolific designer across a range of formats, including posters, book covers, stamps, stained glass, murals and ceramics. His best-known picturebooks are characterized by the use of bold graphic shapes and strong black outlines – as evident, for example, in *The Happy Owls* (1963) and *Celestino Piatti's Animal ABC* (1966). The owl was a constant motif for Piatti, and can be found in his books, posters and other design work. He is quoted as saying, 'You can draw an owl a thousand times and never know its secret.'

   Zirkus Nock is something of an oddity in Piatti's output. The landscape format of the book is used with a basic layout of image facing text across the gutter. The exquisite artwork simply complements the linear story of a circus's arrival, preparation, performance and departure. In many ways, the book is first and foremost a gallery of paintings that can be viewed over and over again.

Zehn Minuten später liegen die Kinder bereits in ihren Bettchen.
Zuweilen trägt der Wind Fetzen von Musik
und das Getrappel der Pferde zu ihnen herüber.
Aber das sind vertraute Geräusche.
Schon schlafen sie friedlich.
Die Mutter streicht zärtlich die Decken glatt
und dann zieht sie sich eilig und ohne die Kinder zu wecken
für die nächste Nummer um.
Der Mond schaut geradewegs in den kleinen Wagen hinein
und lächelt ein wenig.

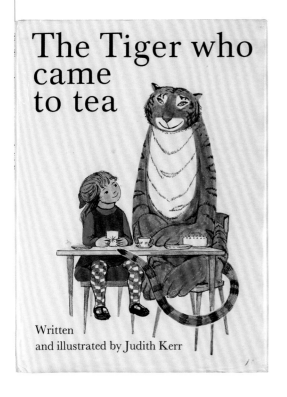

The Tiger who came to tea

Written
and illustrated by Judith Kerr

Sophie's mummy said,
"I wonder who that can be.

It can't be the milkman
because he came this morning

. . . and all the packets and tins in the cupboard

And it can't be the boy from the grocer because this isn't the day he comes.

And it can't be Daddy because he's got his key.

We'd better open the door and see."

The contrasting use of scale and colour makes for an intensely dynamic spread.

And then he looked round the kitchen   to see what else he could find.

58
The Tiger Who Came to Tea

Judith Kerr
Published by William Collins, Sons & Co. Ltd, London, 1968
This copy: 1997 UK edition
(Ted Smart, Godalming, Surrey)
260 x 190 mm (10¼ x 7½ in)

This enduringly successful classic is one of those books whose properties somehow defy analysis. Perhaps its compelling nature must simply be put down to a magical coupling of words and pictures that describe the arrival and departure of a mysterious and magnificent stranger. Kerr's illustrations are mostly loose-edged on the white of the page and are beautifully composed. The abundance of white space in the book gives additional prominence to the single full-bleed, double-page spread that shows the family heading down the street after dark, in search of a restaurant. Inevitably, critics have pointed out the gender stereotyping in the book. But it is very much of its time.

Kerr arrived in the UK as a 10-year-old refugee from Nazi Germany, where her father had been persecuted for his openly expressed views. She has lived in this country ever since and is a naturalized citizen. Her Mog books have also been hugely successful, and she has written acclaimed semi-autobiographical novels that explore a child's flight from pre-war Berlin.

Kerr's work has been celebrated by major UK exhibitions – at the Museum of Childhood in London and at Seven Stories, the National Centre for Children's Books in Newcastle – as well as through the 2013 publication of *Judith Kerr's Creatures: A Celebration of Her Life and Work* (Harper Collins Children's Books).

Peter took a deep breath.
Then he yelled through the pipe,
"Willie—meet us at the parking lot!"
"Head for the parking lot!" one of the big boys yelled.
"Let's go!"

Stencilled lettering, bold composition and theatrical lighting bring a filmic quality to the page.

"Archie, look what I found,"
Peter shouted through the pipe.
"Motorcycle goggles!"
Archie watched Peter through the hole.
He listened, and smiled.

PARKING

Peter, Archie and Willie crept out of the hideout.
When they reached the fence they got up and ran.

The artist exploits rich contrasts between gouache brushstrokes and collaged pattern.

Ezra Jack Keats
Published by Macmillan,
New York, 1969
This copy: 1st edition
(Canada, ex-library)
210 x 235 mm (8¼ x 9¼ in)

Keats's use of the tough, textured world of urban working-class life was unique in contemporary picturebook making. He gave voice to African-American childhood in a way that had not been seen before. In *Goggles!*, Peter and Archie run from a group of older kids who try to take the motorcycle goggles that Peter has found in the wasteland that is their playground. The artist's painterly technique and muted palette, with occasional use of collage, create a rich, oppressive mood.

Keats was born in Brooklyn in 1916, to poor Polish-Jewish immigrant parents. His father's early death curtailed ambitions to study at art school, but Keats eventually studied in Paris for a year in 1949. This was after several years learning the trade as a studio comic-book artist, drawing backgrounds for Captain Marvel strips, and later progressing to drawing characters. After further years of illustrating books by others, he began to create his own. Perhaps the best known is *A Snowy Day*, which won the 1963 Caldecott Medal.

The work of Ezra Jack Keats is preserved as an archive by the de Grummond Children's Literature Collection, at the University of Southern Mississippi; it includes artwork, dummies, roughs and manuscripts for 37 books, as well as personal correspondence. The collection is thoroughly examined and listed by Brian Alderson in his two-volume set, *Ezra Jack Keats: Artist and Picture-book Maker* and *Ezra Jack Keats: A Bibliography and Catalogue* (Pelican, 1994 and 2002).

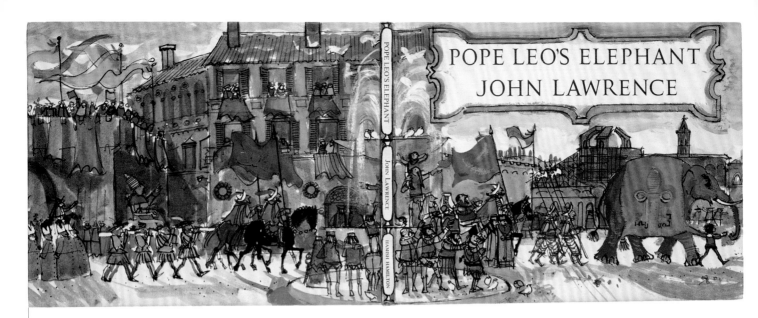

Lawrence weaves a mass of historically accurate visual detail into his recreation of Renaissance Rome.

A combination of accurate line-drawn perspective and vibrant brushwork gives the page movement and drama.

With a mighty snort he sent a stream of water on to the flames.

128

60
Pope Leo's Elephant

John Lawrence
Published by Hamish Hamilton,
London, 1969
This copy: 1st edition
190 x 250 mm (7½ x 10 in)

The work of English illustrator
John Lawrence, most notably his
engravings, has quietly graced
the work of other writers across
six decades; these writers include
Philip Pullman, Charles Causley,
Susan Hill, Allan Ahlberg and Paul
Theroux. His work has matured
and grown over the years, yet
remains fresh and contemporary.

Earlier in his career Lawrence
self-authored a handful of
picturebooks, mostly for Hamish
Hamilton, including this gem.
The idea grew from an article
that he had seen in the Catholic
newspaper *The Tablet*, about Pope
Leo X, who was given an elephant
as a gift. Lawrence immediately
thought that the story could provide
the basis of a picturebook.

As always with Lawrence,
the pictures are underpinned by
careful historical research. The
result combines playful storytelling
and characterization with factual
detail, using a mixture of line, wash
and opaque gouache. The author
builds a narrative around Leophante
the elephant and his young handler,
Paulo. The two are set to work
on the building of the new St
Peter's Basilica. A fire starts in
the woodwork scaffolding and the
elephant saves the day by using his
trunk to carry water and extinguish
the flames.

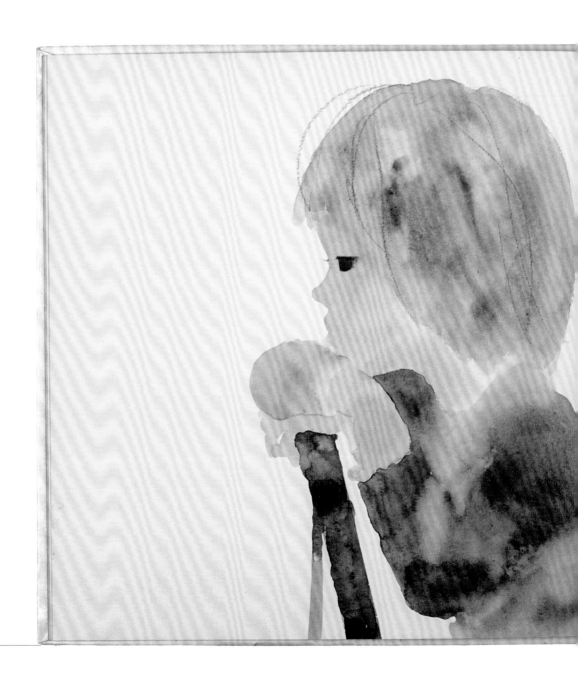

Traditional wet-on-wet watercolour technique is used to describe shapes without outline to evoke the gentle, spiritual tone of the story.

Fumio chased my pretty bird round the garden
with his hat but he could not catch it.

tap! tap! tap!

I am so sad that my pretty bird has gone
but I think he will be happy in the garden with his friends.
There they are at the window.

Chihiro Iwasaki
Published as *Momoko to Kotori*
by Shiko-Sha, Tokyo, 1972
This copy: 1st UK edition
(The Bodley Head, 1972)
250 x 250 mm (10 x 10 in)

Following her death in 1974, the life
and work of Chihiro Iwasaki was
commemorated by the creation of
the Chihiro Iwasaki Art Museum
of Picture Books in Tokyo, built
on the site of Iwasaki's home and
workplace of 22 years. Devoted
to the display of an archive of her
highly popular work, it is one of
the most important collections
of picturebook art in the world. It
is now known as the Chihiro Art
Museum Tokyo. In 1997 a second
site (Chihiro Art Museum Azumino)
was opened in Nagano Prefecture,
the birthplace of Iwasaki's parents,
and both museums have now
received over 2 million visitors.

In her teens Iwasaki studied
drawing and oil painting under
Saburosuke Okada at the Tokyo
School of Fine Arts. Later, she
studied traditional Japanese
calligraphy using ink stick and
brush, a skill that is clearly evident
in the distinctive 'wet on wet'
watercolour technique that she
used in much of her subsequent
illustration work. Iwasaki produced
illustrations for various magazines
and textbooks before receiving
her first big break in 1949, when
the publishing house Doshinsha
invited her to illustrate *Okasan no
hanashi* (The Story of a Mother)
in traditional *kamishibai* ('paper
theatre') form – a tradition of
storytelling using illustrated cards.
Iwasaki's first picturebook, *Hitori de
dekiru yo* (I Can Do it All by Myself),
was published in 1956.

In a quote on the dust jacket
of this edition, the renowned
children's literature critic Margery
Fisher states: 'Japanese artists
have gone further than we have
in offering children a specifically
artistic experience in picture
books; we should be ready to
help our children enjoy this kind
of experience, which they are
often ready for before we realize it.'

And that's what they did.
They built a big strong cage
and popped Mervyn inside.

'I'm a shy sort o
and I don't reall

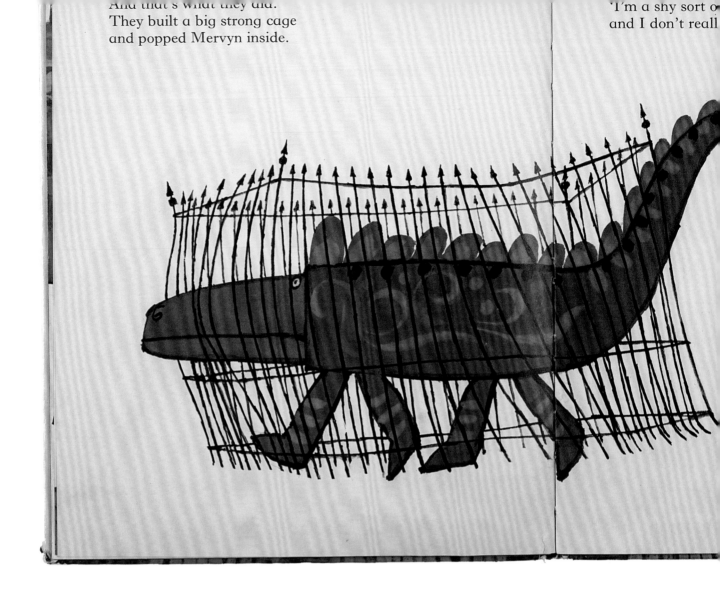

Mervyn started work one Monday morning.
He breathed flames into a funnel
for a solid hour
until the electricity got going.
And he said he quite liked the idea.

'g stared at.'

The author's training and experience as a graphic designer is evident in the elegant balancing of shapes across the page.

62
The Monster from Half-way to Nowhere

Max Velthuijs
Published as *Das gutherzige Ungeheuer* by NordSüd Verlag, Zurich, 1973
This copy: 1st UK edition (A & C Black, London, 1974)
290 x 215 mm (11½ x 8½ in)

Born in The Hague in 1923, Max Velthuijs studied painting and graphic design at the city's Academy of the Visual Arts before working for some time as a graphic all-rounder, designing for advertising, TV and film. He came relatively late to picturebook making, but found great success with the Frog books, beginning with *Frog in Love*, which was championed by the legendary Klaus Flugge at Andersen Press. Flugge went on to publish numerous subsequent titles in the series. Velthuijs's Frog books are characterized by a graphic economy and an ability to address complex existential themes in an elegant, understated manner, always stressing the innate nobility of human kindness.

    The Monster from Half-way to Nowhere was one of the artist's earlier picturebooks, but it already displays Velthuijs's characteristic lightness of touch and quietly philosophical approach. The page designs are masterful both in their use of space and in their distribution of weight and colour. A fire-breathing monster arrives in a village to the consternation of the inhabitants, whose firemen immediately douse him with water. They try to use him as a weapon, but his natural good nature prevents him from wishing harm on anyone. Eventually he is put to work at the newly built power station, where his fire is used to generate electricity for the village.

    Velthuijs received the Hans Christian Andersen Award for his contribution to children's literature in 2004, a year before his death.

Figures are given solid,
static outlines to emphasize
their position in pattern-
based compositions.

Whenever there is a big ceremonial occasion they are always there, controlling the crowds......

Richard and P.C. Downer join the other horses and riders walking along the balcony......

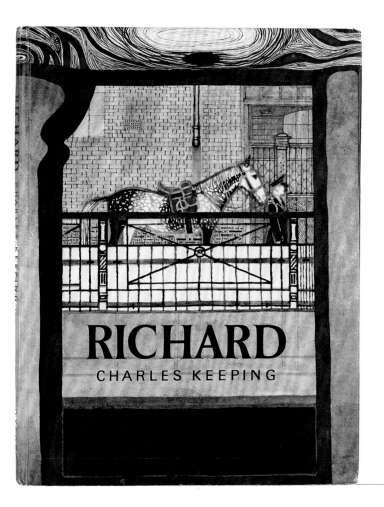

Keeping's expertise in the process of lithography clearly informed his work on *Richard*. Oil-and water-based media collide and separate to create gritty textures.

63
Richard

Charles Keeping
Published by Oxford University Press, London, 1973
This copy: 1st edition
285 x 220 mm (11¼ x 8¾ in)

In contrast to his contemporary John Burningham (see page 113), Keeping was a virtuoso draughtsman. This skill was never more in evidence than when he displayed his understanding of that most difficult of subjects, the horse. (Sir Quentin Blake regularly advises that horses should always be drawn standing in very long grass.) Horses feature prominently in Keeping's work, including his 18 picturebooks. His biographer, Douglas Martin, points out that, 'Since his thematic material was autobiographical at root, he often reveals how a memory retrieved or an incident observed can provide a story-line.'[1]

Richard, like all of Keeping's picturebooks, draws on those retrieved memories and incidents observed while growing up in working-class London and on his passion for horses. In the 1970s, Keeping produced a number of groundbreaking picturebooks that were seen by many at the time as speaking more to adults than to children, but which have become increasingly appreciated over time. Examples are *Through the Window* (1970) and *The Garden Shed* (1971), both with Oxford University Press. Although *Richard* is one of Keeping's more conceptually straightforward picturebooks, and is by no means the best designed, it is a fine example of his love of pattern and texture, and of his ability to juggle these flat shapes with the illusion of depth and space.

or enjoying a trot at the head of the procession.

1   *Charles Keeping: An Illustrator's Life*, by Douglas Martin (Julia MacRae Books, London, 1993).

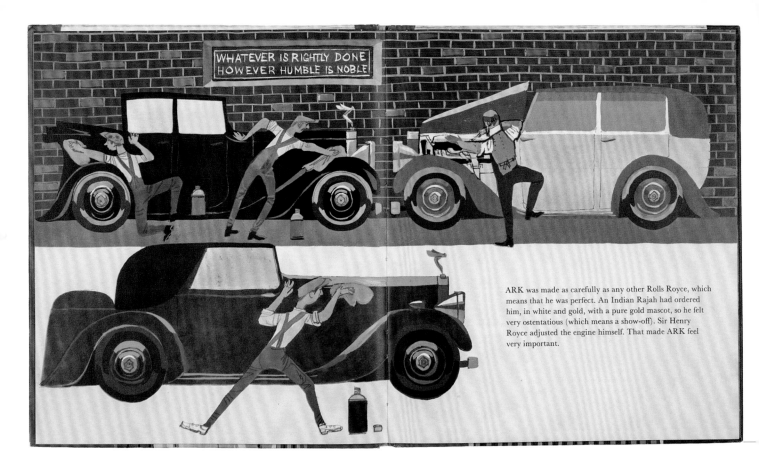

WHATEVER IS RIGHTLY DONE
HOWEVER HUMBLE IS NOBLE

ARK was made as carefully as any other Rolls Royce, which means that he was perfect. An Indian Rajah had ordered him, in white and gold, with a pure gold mascot, so he felt very ostentatious (which means a show-off). Sir Henry Royce adjusted the engine himself. That made ARK feel very important.

Not long afterwards one of the Rajahs sent two thieves to steal ARK. The thieves had only driven lorries before, and they found that the speed of the Rolls took them quite by surprise. Before they knew it they were lost in the jungle and they had to abandon ARK beside a lake.

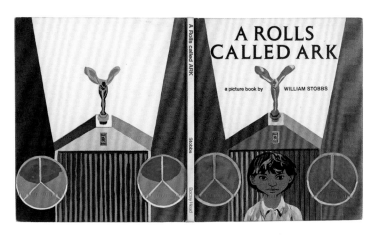

Personal experience as a draughtsman at the Rolls-Royce company informed Stobbs's loving depiction of the cars.

William Stobbs
Published by the Bodley Head, London, 1974
This copy: 1st edition
250 x 220 mm (10 x 8¾ in)

William Stobbs combined a prolific career as a book illustrator with working in the higher echelons of management in British art schools. Born in South Shields, in the north-east of England, he graduated from Durham School of Art in 1938. In the postwar years Stobbs was head of the design department at the London School of Printing and Graphic Arts, and from 1958 to 1979 he was the principal of Maidstone College of Art. Perhaps best known for his exacting, highly graphic black-and-white work (often for non-fiction titles), Stobbs also produced a substantial amount of colour work, including a few self-authored picturebooks.

A Rolls Called Ark drew upon an area of particular interest to Stobbs – cars; more specifically, the Rolls-Royce. He had a collection of these, which would be seen by students (such as this writer) in the art-school car park. Stobbs had worked as a draughtsman at the Rolls-Royce company immediately after graduation, and was involved in the development of the Merlin engine.

This book is the unlikely tale of the adventures of a Rolls that is delivered to a rajah in India. 'Ark was made as carefully as any other Rolls-Royce, which means that he was perfect', Stobbs's text lovingly begins. Painted in gouache, as was much of the illustrative work of this period, and earlier, the images luxuriate in tropical foliage and decoration, with more than a hint of the influence of John Minton (see page 59).

Stobbs's work is characterized by a rich painterly technique and a strong sense of surface design.

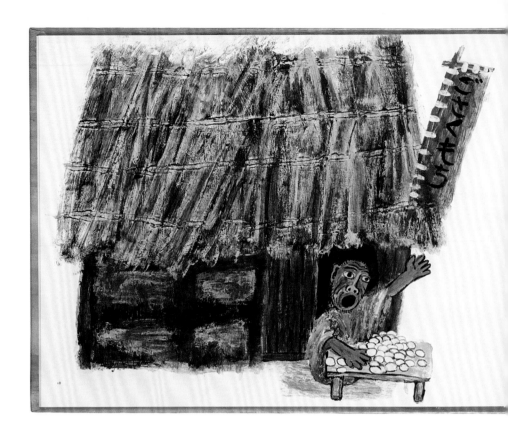

A carefully limited palette of earth colours reflects the rural, traditional context of this Japanese folk tale.

うれたち　うれたち、ごさくは　たちまち　おおがねも

もちごめも　うすも　いらん。あずきを　ちいと　もらってくれば　よい。
あとは、だいふくもちが　こんまい　もちを　こさえてくれる。

これは　うまい　かねもうけに　なると、ごさくは　おもうた。
なまけものの　ごさくにしては　えらい　はりきって　みせを　だした。
まずは、もちずきの　おしょうが　かいにきた。

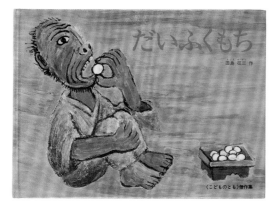

Vigorous brushwork and a childlike approach to perspective lend a raw, edgy feel to the book.

**Daifuku Mochi
(The Strange Rice Cake)**

Seizo Tashima
Published by Fukuinkan Shoten,
Tokyo, 1976
This copy: later edition (2006)
195 x 270 mm (7¾ x 10½ in)

The creative works of Japanese artist Seizo Tashima span picturebooks, sculpture and installation. His 3D works are made with such natural materials as bamboo, nuts and driftwood. In 2009 he collaborated with members of a rural community in Niigata Prefecture to create an installation (*Museum of Picture Book Art*) that celebrated the life of the abandoned local school that housed it.

Born in 1940 in Osaka, Tashima studied painting at Tama Art University in Tokyo. His first picturebook, *Shibaten*, was created during his studies and published much later, in 1971, by Kaisei-sha. Tashima's books have become an institution in Japan, and he has received numerous national awards for his work, as well as international acclaim at both the Bologna and Bratislava book fairs.

The Strange Rice Cake is a traditional cautionary tale that tells of the perils and consequences of greed. Tashima's primitive, muscular paintwork heightens the traditional folk-art feel of the book, and the crude depiction of facial expressions creates a highly theatrical sense of melodrama.

Various visual jokes are
played out in identical
colours on each spread
to the ongoing rhythmic
chant of the text below.

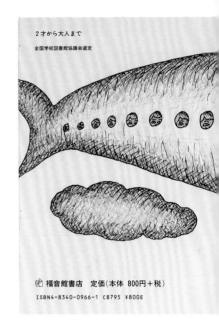

２才から大人まで

全国学校図書館協議会選定

福音館書店　定価（本体　800円＋税）

ISBN4-8340-0966-1 C8795 ¥800E

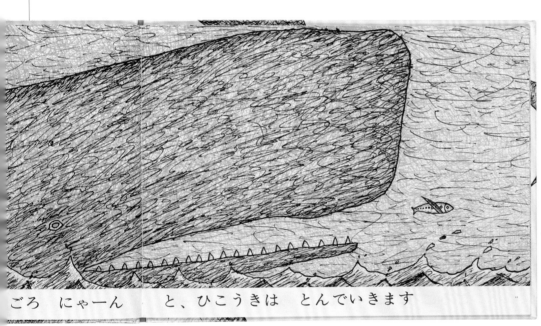

ごろ　にゃーん　　　　と、ひこうきは　とんでいきます

ごろごろ　にゃー

ごろ、ねこたちは　　　にゃーん　にゃーん　ないています

ごろごろ　にゃー

140

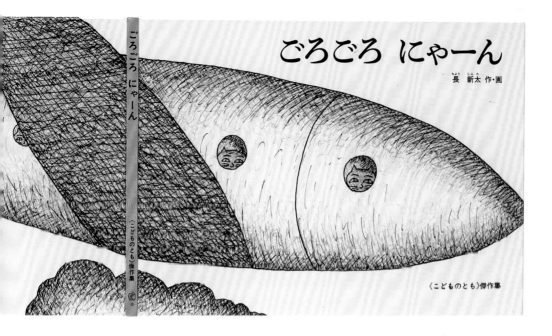

ごろごろ にゃーん

長 新太 作・画

《こどものとも》傑作集

ごろ にゃーん と、ひこうきは とんでいきます

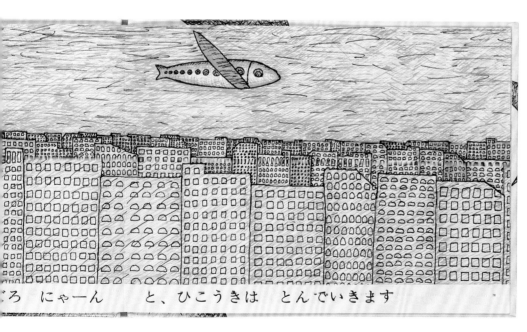

ろ にゃーん と、ひこうきは とんでいきます

Shinta Cho
Published by Fukuinkan Shoten,
Tokyo, 1976
This copy: later Japanese reprint
195 x 265 mm (7¾ x 10½ in)

The Japanese artist Shinta Cho died in 2005 at the age of 78. His over inventive and varied work is much loved in his home country. A native of Tokyo, Cho first found a job as a graphic artist on a Tokyo newspaper by winning a cartoon competition in 1948. After achieving some success as a manga artist, he left the newspaper to forge a freelance career. His books have won numerous awards in Japan and further afield, one of his best-known being *The Gas We Pass: The Story of Farts* (1991), which has delighted and reassured children of several generations, and which the *New York Times* reported had sold 380,000 copies in English by 1997.

Adventurous Flying of Cats sees Cho at his most nonsensical and playful. A verbal description of the plot is an inevitably reductive exercise, as the book depends very much on the sounds of words, which children delight in repeating. These begin with the rhythmic chants of a group of cats, who are rowing their rubber rafts towards a flying-fish-shaped plane, floating on the water: 'With a gorogoro nyaan, gorogoro nyaan …'

Drawn with a childlike and crudely scribbled hatching, the surreal journey continues, with the cats encountering a huge whale, a flying saucer and a snake that fills the page, until finally the plane lands back on the ocean and, 'with a gorogoro nyaan, gorogoro nyaan', the cats row away from their craft.

The landscape format of the book is used to emphasize the shape of the train and its journey from right to left – the traditional way in which Japanese books are laid out.

Panning back to give a sense of the vastness of the station hall, the artist introduces us to the family as they set off on their journey.

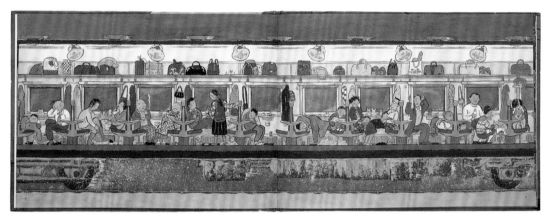

67
Yako Ressha (Night train)

Shigeo Nishimura
Published by Fukuinkan Shoten,
Tokyo, 1980
This copy: 1st edition
195 x 265 mm (7¾ x 10½ in)

Born in 1947 in Kochi, Japan,
Nishimura has for many years
created books that are much loved
in his native country. He specializes
in descriptive picturebooks that
abound with the details of everyday
human activity. He has received a
number of prestigious awards, such
as the Japan Picturebook Award
for *An Illustrated History of Japan*
(1985), and the Sankei Children's
Book Award for *Hiroshima: A
Tragedy Never to be Repeated*
(1995; text by Masamoto Nasu).
    Yako Ressha follows the journey
of a mother and father and their
two children, one a baby. On the
opening page we are introduced
to them visually, isolated against
the white of the page alongside
the titles. Reading right to left, we
turn the page to find ourselves in
an enormous station hall, thronging
with travellers. Our family is
instantly findable in the crowd as
they head towards the platform.
From here onwards, each spread
continues in its long, landscape
format, showing the train at exactly
the same scale page by page,
on its journey as we observe the
passengers and their activities in
cut-out. We follow charming mini-
narratives of other passengers as
time goes by: people prepare for
sleep in different ways, depending
on what kind of compartment they
are in; dad takes the little boy to
the toilet; mum changes a nappy
as the train continues its journey
through the snow. Gradually,
everyone begins to prepare for
arrival at the final destination.
All of this takes place against a
backdrop of carefully researched
technical detail. It is not hard to
see why the book has achieved
enduring popularity.

r looking,
obber caves,
n off the sea
song:

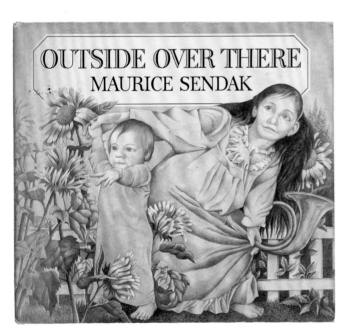

144

When Papa was away at sea,

"Terrible Ida," the goblins said,
"we're dancing sick and must to bed."

But Ida played a frenzied jig, a hornpipe
that makes sailors wild beneath the ocean moon.

Maurice Sendak
Published by Harper & Row,
New York, 1981
This copy: 1st UK edition
(The Bodley Head, 1981)
235 x 255 mm (9¼ x 10 in)

Named as a Caldecott Honor
Book after its publication, this
is one of Sendak's most famous
and most controversial books.
Sendak made it clear that he did
not write 'for children'. He just
wrote. Indeed, he stated that he
did not acknowledge the concept
of 'childhood' as a separate state.
He spoke about this in an interview
that was recorded in 2009 for a
documentary by Lance Bangs
and Spike Jonze, the title of which
– *Tell Them Anything You Want:
A Portrait of Maurice Sendak* –
reflects Sendak's approach.

In *Outside Over There*, the great
picturebook master tells the story
of Ida, who watches over her baby
sister while papa is away at sea.
But the hooded goblins come and
take baby away, leaving an ice baby
in her place who melts away in
Ida's arms. In her search for baby,
Ida climbs backwards out of the
window into the world of Outside
Over There. Sendak creates a
magnificent, dense, haunting world,
which is rendered in the intense
detail and manner of European
Romanticism, each image in the
form of a tableau.

The book was inspired by the
sensational case of the kidnapping
of aviator Charles Lindbergh's baby
son in 1932; Sendak remembered
seeing the story in the newspapers
at the age of 4. The book has
become an enduring classic,
though at the time of its publication,
and subsequently, many have
criticized the book as too disturbing
for children.

and Mama in the arbor,

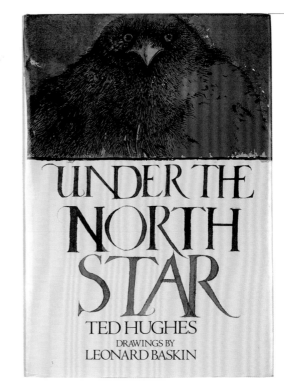

Baskin's calligraphic watercolour lettering naturally complements his paintings.

Each spread features a dramatic full-page animal portrait as a visual counterpoint to, rather than an illustration of, each of Hughes's poems.

THE GRIZZLY BEAR

I see a bear
Growing out of a bulb in wet soil licks its black tip
With a pink tongue its little eyes
Open and see a present an enormous bulging mystery
    package
Over which it walks sniffing at seams
Digging at the wrapping overjoyed holding the joy off
    sniffing and scratching
Teasing itself with scrapings and lickings and the thought
    of it
And little sips of the ecstasy of it

O bear do not open your package
Sit on your backside and sunburn your belly
It is all there it has actually arrived
No matter how long you dawdle it cannot get away
Shamble about lazily laze there in the admiration of it
With all the insects it's attracted all going crazy
And those others the squirrel with its pop-eyed amazement
The deer with its pop-eyed incredulity
The weasel pop-eyed with envy and trickery
All going mad for a share wave them off laze
Yawn and grin let your heart thump happily
Warm your shining cheek fur in the morning sun

You have got it everything for nothing

30

THE SNOWY OWL

Yellow Eye O Yellow Eye
Yellow as the yellow Moon.

Out of the Black Hole of the North
The Ice Age is flying!

The Moon is flying low—
The Moon looms, hunting her Hare—

The Moon drops down, big with frost
And hungry as the end of the world.

The North Pole, rusty-throated,
Screeches, and the globe shudders—

The globe's eyes have squeezed shut with fear.
But the stars are shaking with joy.

And look!

The Hare has a dazzling monument!
A big-eyed blizzard standing

On feet of black iron!
Let us all rejoice in the Hare!

Snowy Owl O Snowy Owl
Staring the globe to stillness!

The Moon flies up.

A white mountain is flying.

The Hare has become an angel!

16

Ted Hughes, illustrated by
Leonard Baskin
Published by Faber & Faber,
London/Boston, 1981
This copy: 1st edition
285 x 200 mm (11¼ x 8 in)

In a conversation between Ted
Hughes and Leonard Baskin that
was recorded by photographer
and friend of both Noel Chanan
in 1983, and which forms the basis
of Chanan's 2009 documentary
about the pair, Baskin describes
their long-standing working
relationship as an 'affinity' – 'a
relationship of presence', rather
than 'a relationship of influence'.
Baskin was dismissive of the idea
of 'illustration' in the context of
such poetry as that of Hughes, and
saw theirs as an almost symbiotic
relationship, wherein the two
created parallel worlds of verbal
and visual poetry in such books
as *Crow* (1970) and *Cave Birds*
(1978), both for Faber & Faber.

Baskin was born in New
Brunswick, New Jersey, and lived
most of his life in the US. For a
number of years, however, he chose
to live and work in the UK, close
to Hughes's home in Devon. He
taught printmaking and sculpture
at Smith College in Northampton,
Massachusetts, from 1953 to 1974
(the year he moved to England). His
1973 book *Hosie's Alphabet* was
one of the Caldecott Honor Books
of that year.

In 1979 Hughes and Baskin
undertook a shared trip to what
Baskin described as the 'honest-
to-god wilderness' of Baxter State
Park in Maine. It was this trip that
inspired *Under the North Star*. The
artist and poet created responses
to the various species that inhabit
the wilderness.

1   *The Artist and the Poet: Leonard Baskin
    & Ted Hughes in Conversation 1983*,
    by Noel Chanan, 2009.

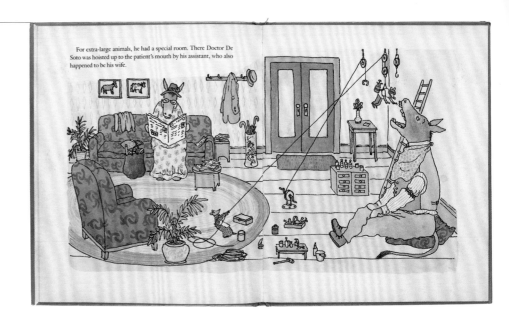

For extra-large animals, he had a special room. There Doctor De
Soto was hoisted up to the patient's mouth by his assistant, who also
happened to be his wife.

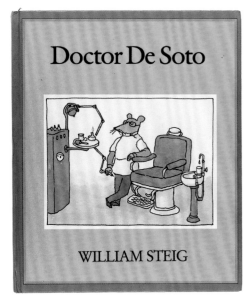

Doctor De Soto

WILLIAM STEIG

Doctor De Soto climbed up the ladder and bravely entered the
fox's mouth. "Ooo-wow!" he gasped. The fox had a rotten bicuspid
and unusually bad breath.

"This tooth will have to come out," Doctor De Soto announced.
"But we can make you a new one."

When the dentist was done, he stepped out. "Now close your jaws tight," he said, "and keep them closed for a full minute." The fox did as he was told. Then he tried to open his mouth—but his teeth were stuck together!

"Ah, excuse me, I should have mentioned," said Doctor De Soto, "you won't be able to open your mouth for a day or two. The secret formula must first permeate the dentine. But don't worry. No pain ever again!"

The fox was stunned. He stared at Doctor De Soto, then at his wife. They smiled, and waited. All he could do was say, "Frank oo berry mush" through his clenched teeth, and get up and leave. He tried to do so with dignity.

"Just stop the pain," whimpered the fox, wiping some tears away.
Despite his misery, he realized he had a tasty little morsel in his mouth, and his jaw began to quiver. "Keep open!" yelled Doctor De Soto. "Wide open!" yelled his wife.

William Steig
Published by Farrar, Straus and Giroux, New York, 1982
This copy: 1st UK edition (Andersen Press, London, 1983)
255 x 215 mm (10 x 8½ in)

Steig died in 2003 at the age of 95 after an illustrious career as a humourist, writer and illustrator. He started working as a cartoonist at an early age and produced more than 1600 drawings and 117 covers for the *New Yorker* magazine alone. All are characterized by his highly distinctive, sardonic sense of humour. Steig did not begin making picturebooks until he was into his sixties. Of these it is *Shrek!* that has become the most widely known in recent years, thanks to the success of the Hollywood films based on it. *Sylvester and the Magic Pebble*, the Caldecott Medal-winning story of Sylvester the donkey's discovery of a magic pebble that can make wishes come true, has also become a classic. It caused some controversy on publication, however, as Steig had cast pigs as police, a derogatory association that was particularly prevalent in the 1960s when the book came out. Although Steig insisted that no offence had been intended, the book was banned in some places.

As with all of Steig's books, *Doctor De Soto* is firmly underpinned by a profound and meaningful narrative delivered with a lightness of touch and great humour. A fox is suffering from acute toothache and begs the dentists, who happen to be mice, to remove the painful tooth. Despite their stated policy of 'Cats and other dangerous animals not accepted for treatment', the mice take pity on him and perform an extraction. As Steig's text reveals, the fox himself is similarly torn: 'On his way home, he wondered if it would be shabby of him to eat the De Sotos when the job was done.'

At school young Charles did very well
And quickly learnt to read and spell.
He earned himself the teachers' praise
With addings-up and take-aways.
At work or sport he did his best
And seemed to rise above the rest.

Charles and his friend, Amelia Gwen,
Soon arranged to meet again,
And so they did, and found that they
Were meeting almost every day.
Their friendship slowly turned to love
And they got married (see above).

A taste for the absurd is evident in all of Gerrard's compositions.

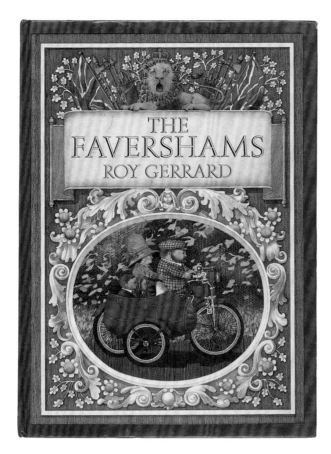

Gerrard's masterful command of the highly technical medium of watercolour augments the deeply English, Victorian flavour of the book.

71
The Favershams

Roy Gerrard
Published by Victor Gollancz, London, 1982
This copy: 1st edition
284 x 207 mm (11¼ x 8 in)

Gerrard is something of a forgotten genius whose work is beginning to be reappraised. His career as a picturebook maker was relatively short. He started late, having worked as an art teacher for many years, alongside his work as a painter in oils, and died suddenly from a heart attack at the age of 62. In an autobiographical note at the back of *The Favershams*, Gerrard writes: 'In 1972 I was immobilized for several weeks after a climbing accident, and I started tinkering around with small watercolours. My painting became obsessive and gradually took up all my spare time. In about three years I finally arrived at my true style of painting: small, highly detailed watercolours, remorselessly whimsical, and often Victorian/Edwardian in subject.'

This unique, beautifully crafted world of earnest, tubby characters is perhaps at its best in *The Favershams*. The artist's exacting watercolour technique never wavers in its detailed exploration of surface pattern in interiors, clothing or foliage, and it is indeed 'remorselessly whimsical'. The illustrations are, in turn, propelled by Gerrard's own charming rhyming couplets.

Charles took some time off for a while
To shoot a wicked crocodile
Which chewed up people by the score.
(They say it swallowed ninety-four.)
And all those who had not been chewed
Came round to show their gratitude.

A farm in the country is a quiet place with lots of space.
Your nearest neighbor's house may be a mile or more away. Though not so many people live here, those who do will be good friends to you. Everyone will know your name.
And if there's no one about to talk to, there is always something worth looking at.

Beside your house there are barns and stables and toolsheds and tractorsheds.
There are fields and fences and streams and trees.
You can see an amazing amount of sky.
But a farm in the country is not quite as deserted and quiet as it seems.

Some days your mother will pick you up after school if you have a dentist's appointment or you need new shoes. Then you have a chance to spend some time in the nearest small town. There is only one main street with shops but it has a clothes shop and a variety store and a bank. You can buy some candy or an ice cream or a book in the drug store. You can buy nails and paint and tools and string in the hardware shop.

There are lots of things you do grow tho
You can buy vegetable seeds or seedling
and radishes, onions and cabbages and
your garden. When you preserve your ow
from your own strawberries, everything

Even if your room
is on the top floor
of a big apartment house,
long after you are fast asleep
the lights of the city
will be shining on your ceiling.

A big city stays awake all night.
Neon signs blink on and off.
Traffic signals change from red to green.
Late buses stop and go.
Doormen whistle.
A taxi horn honks.

People are in the streets,
laughing and singing and shouting.

Far in the distance,
a siren answers a fire alarm.
A tugboat toots
Underground, the trains rumble.

It is surprising how easy it is to sleep
through the sounds of a crowded city
if you are used to them.
But once in a while,
if you are wakeful,
you may imagine an underground railway
taking you out of the city to
a quiet place with lots of space.

Alice and Martin Provensen
Published by Crown Publishers
Inc., New York, 1984
This copy: 1st UK edition
(Jonathan Cape, 1984)
320 x 230 mm (12½ x 9 in)

'You see, we were a true collaboration. Martin and I really were one artist.' So said Alice Provensen, speaking after Martin's death in 1987, about their work as a team. The nature of their respective roles has intrigued many, but has never been entirely revealed. Prior to meeting in 1943, the pair had led remarkably parallel lives, each having been born in Chicago and having moved to California at the age of 12. They both also studied at the Art Institute of Chicago and the University of California, and both subsequently worked in animation – Alice at the Walter Lantz studio and Martin with Disney. Later, in 1952, Martin created the famous Kellogg's advertising character, Tony the Tiger.

As a book-making team, the two created a highly distinctive 'brand', across many years of making award-winning picturebooks. The visual language perhaps owes something to such artists as Ben Shahn (see page 83), but also to broader traditions of American folk art and popular culture.

The couple moved to New York City after World War II, and later lived for many years at Maple Hill Farm in Dutchess County, upstate New York, which inspired *The Year at Maple Hill Farm* in 1978. *Town and Country* is, as its dust jacket explains, 'an evocation of 33 years of commuting between this country home and New York City. In it, the Provensens express their deep affection for both kinds of living.'

The Provensens take evident delight in describing the textures of everyday life in town and country, creating a flat, largely perspective-free pattern of town and country living.

nd apples and all kinds of vegetables.
y—lettuce and carrots and beans
ing tastes so good when it is fresh from
ars or in the deep-freeze, or make jam
exception of turnips)

witch.
in a great
. When you
dog sitting
ry about
t to you—
s you want
have silver,
chest, a
the same
with silver.
he dog
ch is as big
e apron and

At once
king and
tumbled
were terri
king and

Hutton's economic and understated technique relied heavily on a strong understanding of light.

THE
TINDERBOX

HANS CHRISTIAN ANDERSEN
ILLUSTRATED BY WARWICK HUTTON

Soon

judge, the councillors, and the
them up in the air and as they
hed to pieces. The soldiers
le shouted, "You shall be our
rincess!"

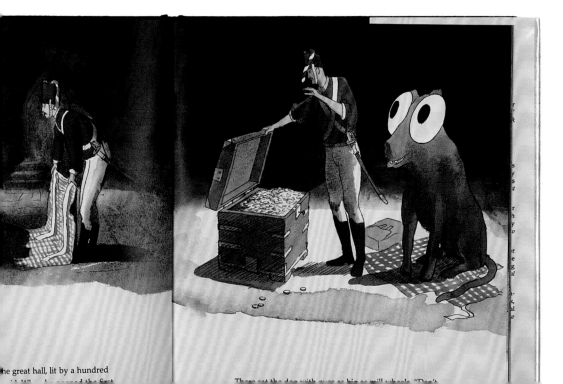

he great hall, lit by a hundred

Hans Christian Andersen,
illustrated by Warwick Hutton
Published by Macmillan,
New York, 1988
This copy: 1st edition
280 x 215 mm (11 x 8½ in)

Warwick Hutton's picturebooks
tended to use folk tales, mythology
and Bible stories as their
inspiration. Among the books that
he made before his tragically early
death in 1994, at the age of just 55,
were two that featured in the *New
York Times* annual Best Illustrated
Children's Books list: *The Nose
Tree* (1981) and *Jonah and the
Great Fish* (1983), which also won
the Boston Globe–Horn Book
Award for 1984.

Hutton was born into an artistic
family. His father was the artist
and glass engraver John Hutton,
whose work graces great buildings
around the world, but who is
particularly celebrated for his
designs for the Great West Screen
of Coventry Cathedral, which took
ten years to complete. Warwick
taught illustration for many years
at Cambridge School of Art (now
part of Anglia Ruskin University),
but his books were rather better
appreciated in the US than in his
native England.

The Tinderbox features all the
artist's familiar characteristics – a
strong eye for light and shadow, a
keen interest in pattern and surface
decoration, and a hesitant yet
nevertheless deliberate line. The
illustrations are classical, elegant
and always respectful of the text,
but with a hint of the grotesque.
Andersen's dog with 'eyes as large
as the Round Tower' is a sinister
presence in the darkness of the
artist's fluid washes.

He stood there for quite a long time, thinking of his fate, and at last his father
asked him, "Do you fancy any of my work, young sir? A pair of new slippers,
or perhaps," he added with a smile, "a case to cover up your nose?"
"What do you mean, my nose?" asked Jacob. "Why would I need a case for it?"
"Well, everyone to his own taste!" replied the cobbler. "But I must say, if I had a

terrible nose like that, I'd cover it up with a case of pink patent leather. Look,
I have a nice piece right here, although I'd need a pretty good length to make
you such a case. But think how well protected you'd be, young sir! As things
are, I'm sure you must bump into every doorway, and try to avoid every
carriage."
Jacob stood there dumb with horror; he felt his nose—it was thick, and as long
as his two hands. So the old woman had changed his shape, too!
That was why his mother didn't know him. That was why people called him
an ugly dwarf! "Master," he asked the cobbler, almost weeping, "do you have
a mirror here where I could see my reflection?"
"Young sir," said his father earnestly, "you aren't exactly blessed with the
kinds of looks calculated to make you vain, and there's no call for you to
keep looking in the mirror every hour or so. You ought to break yourself of
the habit! In you of all people, it's ridiculous."
"Oh, do let me look in a mirror," cried Jacob. "It's not out of vanity,
I promise you!"

18 19

did credit to his
ed man since Dwarf
fit to fling the dishes
ven threw a rather
r Cook himself—so
to spend three days in
veral handfuls of
ed up his food without

ged as if by magic. The
his smallest servant's
r. No, he thought
od-tempered, and he
ook and Dwarf Nose
e of them sit on his
s of the choice dishes in
ey both valued at its

he Chief Master Cook's
e distinguished
take lessons from the
e sum of money, for
f the cooks happy, and
the money the

years. To all outward
only the thought of
d to him until the
y clever and lucky in

32 33

74
Dwarf Nose

Wilhelm Hauff, illustrated by
Lisbeth Zwerger
Published as *Der Zwerg Nase* by
Michael Neugebauer Verlag AG,
Gossau, Zurich, 1993
This copy: 1st English-language
edition (North South Books/
Michael Neugebauer, New York,
1994)
275 x 230 mm (11 x 9 in)

Wilhelm Hauff's tale of a market
boy who dares to reprimand an old
woman for touching his herbs and
cabbages, and who is then turned
by her into a long-nosed dwarf,
provides the perfect vehicle for
Zwerger's unique visual language.
The story's original German title
was *Der Zwerg Nase* (Little Long-
nose), and it was one of the many
fairy tales that Hauff wrote in his
short life (he died in 1827 at the
age of 25). His tales are still popular
in German-speaking countries.

The illustrations of Vienna-based
Zwerger have been recognized
by numerous awards and medals
over the years, including the Hans
Christian Andersen Award in
1990. Specializing in fairy tales,
she combines a darkly imaginative
vision with exceptional technical
skill in that most difficult of media,
watercolour. Zwerger is one of
the few illustrators working today
whose levels of draughtsmanship
and craft skill make her comparable
to the greats of the Golden Age
of children's illustration, such
as Edmund Dulac and Arthur
Rackham, whose work was a key
influence in persuading her to
pursue illustration as a career after
studying painting in Vienna. Michael
Neugebauer has been a champion
of her work for many years, and
here he publishes Zwerger at
her best.

Pacovská uses the book as
a stage on which to explore
colour, form and sound.

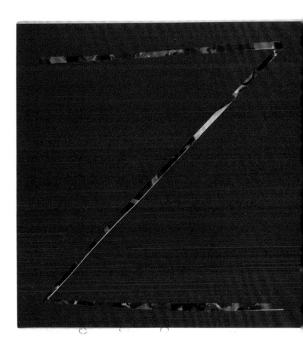

Intense, sensual reds
invariably dominate
Pacovská's book work.

Kvêta Pacovská
Published by Ravensburger
Buchverlag Otto Maier,
Ravensburg, Germany, 1994
This copy: 2012 UK edition
(Tate Publishing, London)
250 x 250 mm (10 x 10 in)

Pacovská has been a leading
innovator in the picturebook field
for many decades. Her work defies
categorization and freely straddles
illustration, book arts, sculpture
and installation. Born in Prague in
1928, she attended the Academy of
Applied Arts in that city, graduating
in 1952. In her picturebooks,
Pacovská embraces space, colour
and form. She always explores and
plays with the physical make-up
of the book as an object, as a total
experience that is not rooted in the
visualization of text or narrative.

In a 2001 interview with Wendy
Coates-Smith for the journal *Line*,
Pacovská spoke of the relationship
between colour and sound: 'Colour.
White and black are not included in
the colour spectrum but for me they
are colours and mean maximum
contrast. And maximum contrast is
the maximum beauty. I am striving
for maximum contrast. Red and
green. The placing of colours, one
over the other. It depends on the
relation; proportion, rhythm, size,
amount and how we place colours
together. It is like music. Each
individual tone is beautiful by itself
and in certain groupings we can
create new dimensions – harmony,
disharmony, symphonies, operas
and books for children.'[1]

1 *Line*, volume 2 (APU, Cambridge, 2001).

Erlbruch's highly unusual use of mixed media is held together by a strong sense of design and colour.

Subtle surreal influences from such artists as Giorgio de Chirico and Odilon Redon are evident.

Or, dans le pays, on commença
à se méfier de cette femme qui
toujours s'approchait des mouflets,
les scrutait et les tâtait avec
des mains avides, et des airs…
qui vous faisaient courir un frisson
dans le dos. La rumeur se répandit
que, quoi qu'elle voulût aux petits,
mieux valait les garder au logis.
Et la maraudeuse eut la surprise,
passant par les villages et les villes,
de ne plus rien voir trotter
qui mesurât moins d'un mètre.
Elle en fut fort fâchée.
– Les imbéciles ! se dit-elle
en maugréant. C'est qu'ils veulent
me pousser à la méchanceté.
S'ils le prennent comme cela,
ce n'est pas un que je leur croquerai,
mais mille et un !

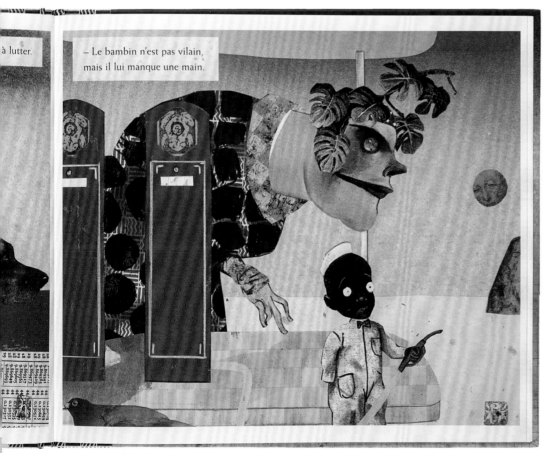

à lutter.

– Le bambin n'est pas vilain,
mais il lui manque une main.

76
L'Ogresse en pleurs
(The crying ogress)

Valérie Dayre, illustrated by
Wolf Erlbruch
Published by Éditions Milan,
Toulouse, 1996
This copy: 1st edition
250 x 285 mm (10 x 11½ in)

Not many picturebooks open with
the words, 'There was once a
woman so bad that she dreamt of
eating a child.' Dayre's wonderful
text is perfectly complemented
by Wolf Erlbruch's highly original,
uncompromising artwork.
Erlbruch's ogress is truly terrifying,
filling the first spread with her
enormous bulk, jutting jaw and
headdress of Swiss cheese plants.
This is an artist who has never
shied away from confrontation, and
who refuses to patronize children
– an attitude typified by his much-
acclaimed *Duck, Death and the
Tulip*, which explores the subject
of death as a life-long companion.
In fact Erlbruch does not like to
be characterized as a children's
book illustrator at all, preferring
to allow his books to find their own
audience, whatever age it might
be. Despite this, the artist received
the prestigious Hans Christian
Andersen Award in 2006.

Erlbruch uses a range of media,
always experimenting and always
led by concept ahead of style.
Here he seems to be using almost
every medium under the sun –
transparent washes, colour pencils,
paint and collage among them
– yet they are perfectly integrated
and held together by a carefully
considered colour palette.

Erlbruch studied graphic design
in Essen from 1967 to 1974.
Alongside his work as an artist he
is also a professor of illustration at
the University of Wuppertal.

The wide landscape format of the book is perfectly suited to Fanelli's free-flowing multiple narratives.

Double-page images give way to comic-book format sequential spreads.

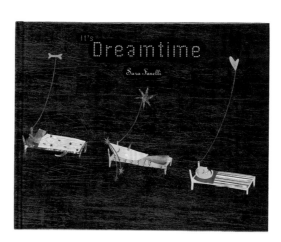

Sara Fanelli
Published by Heinemann Young
Books, London, 1999
This copy: 1st edition
243 x 304 mm (9½ x 12 in)

Fanelli's highly distinctive work
in picturebooks has played an
important role in influencing the
evolution of the form. Born in
Florence, she came to the UK to
study at Camberwell College of
Arts; she then graduated from the
Royal College of Art in 1995. While
studying, she won the Macmillan
Prize for children's picturebook
illustration for her first book, *Button*,
which was published in 1993 by
Walker Books. In the ensuing years,
as well as producing a stream of
beautiful picturebooks, Fanelli has
worked on projects with both Tate
Modern and Tate Britain in London,
and on books for Tate Publishing
and Phaidon that showcase her
work to a wider age group.

It's Dreamtime was perhaps
too graphically complex to
achieve commercial success
in the children's publishing arena,
but Fanelli's experimentation on
the borders between traditional
picturebook structure and graphic
novel/comic conventions was way
ahead of its time. As an artefact
or *livre d'artiste*, it is as stunning
today as it seemed on publication
in 1999. The artist's use of half-
tone screens within the sequential
comic-format spreads harks
back to mid-twentieth-century
print processes, where crude,
low-density half-tones and cheap
paper were used to save money.
Three characters and their three
dreams are woven together using
a melange of texture, colour, word
and image.

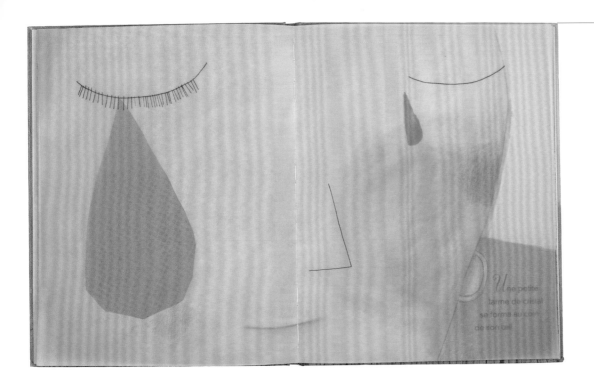

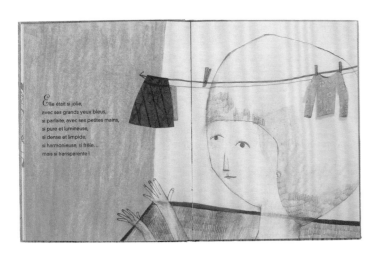

Mais tout cela ne préoccupait pas la petite Gisèle. C'était plutôt autre chose qui l'inquiétait.

Gisèle de verre (Glass Gisèle)

Beatrice Alemagna
Published by Seuil Jeunesse,
Paris, 2002
This copy: 1st edition
265 x 215 mm (10½ x 8½ in)

This multi-award-winning picturebook maker is well known throughout much of Europe and the Far East, but is only now beginning to penetrate the English-language market (see also page 185). Beatrice Alemagna's books can be profound, playful or lyrical, but they are always beautiful. *Gisèle de verre* is a particularly poetic example that tells of a girl born with transparent skin. Everyone can see through her, and all of her thoughts are visible to the world. When she was a child, this charming trait draws admiration and wonder. People travel from far and wide to see, and see through, her. But as she grows towards adulthood, her transparency becomes less charming and more challenging to the sensibilities of the chattering classes: '"You cannot possibly think that? Are you not ashamed of such horrors?" they declare. Pure and luminous, frail and transparent, Gisèle packed her case, hugged her parents and left.'

The ever-inventive Alemagna uses transparent vellum paper to great effect as she tells the story, the form of the book becoming inseparable from its content. The binding-in of printed vellum sheets gives the book an extra dimension. The artist needed to design pages that could be read from multiple viewpoints, which created complex and challenging compositional problems, as shapes and colours show through the vellum from the next or previous page. This is managed masterfully, with content rather than gimmick always retaining priority.

Mais pendant que maman
était dans la cuisine,
je suis sorti sur le balcon et,
à toute vitesse,
j'ai fait une boule de neige.

Demain ?
Demain…

The lack of tonal contrast describes the silent, snowy world perfectly.

79
Jour de neige
(Snow day)

Komako Sakaï
Published by L'École des Loisirs,
Paris, 2006
This copy: 2008 Lutin Poche
edition
190 x 150 mm (7½ x 6 in)

The Japanese artist Komako Sakaï
studied at Tokyo University of the
Arts and went on to design kimonos
and other traditional textiles before
turning to picturebook making. *Jour
de neige* tells the story of a child
who wakes up one morning to find
the world covered in snow and
school closed, an exciting event
that will be familiar to many small
children. What makes this book so
special is the artist's understated
use of colour, and the way in which
the adventure is seen and told
through the eyes and words of the
child. We barely notice that the
characters at the centre of things,
living in a high-rise apartment,
are rabbits.

Sakaï's painterly artwork
perfectly captures the silent, heavy
world of falling snow. The sense
of cold and darkness is palpable
and expressed with minimal fuss
or detail – just broad brushstrokes
and an intense understanding
of light.

Sakaï first came to prominence
with *Yoru kuma* (Night Bear) in
1999, and many of her subsequent
books have been translated into
other languages, including *Emily's
Balloon* (2006) and *The Fox God*
(text by Kimiko Aman, 2003). Sakaï
has received numerous awards for
her work, including a BIB Plaque
for *Friday Sugar* at the 2005
Biennial of Illustrations Bratislava,
and a Dutch Zilveren Griffel (Silver
Pencil) in 2006 for *Mad at Mommy*.

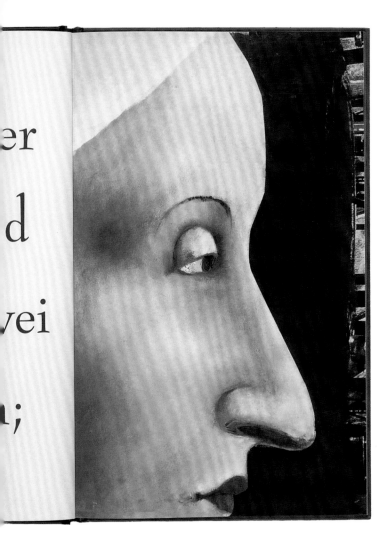

Photographic collage is successfully integrated with elements painted in oil, thanks to careful control of the overall colour balance.

Susanne Janssen's richly sensual use of paint and colour creates a dramatic, theatrical version of this well-known tale.

80
Hänsel und Gretel (Hansel and Gretel)

Adapted and illustrated by
Susanne Janssen
Published by Hinstorff, Rostock,
Germany, 2007
This copy: 1st edition
350 x 220 mm (14 x 8¾ in)

Susanne Janssen and the Brothers Grimm form a natural partnership. Janssen's artwork is created at a large scale, often measuring up to 2 metres (6½ feet) in height. She employs a mixture of collage and oil painting to create dark, unsettling imagery that is best conveyed through books that are produced to a large format, such as this one.

Janssen studied graphic design in Düsseldorf, where she was a pupil of Wolf Erlbruch (see page 161). She was also influenced by the Italian masters of the Renaissance, an influence that presents itself in the fresco-like effect of much of her work. In *Hänsel und Gretel*, Janssen employs a limited range of dark colours – predominantly reds and greys – in a highly theatrical and psychological interpretation that focuses on the sadness inherent in this well-known tale.

This is a book for all ages. Janssen's uncompromising artwork will perhaps not be to the taste of those who hold strong views about what is or is not appropriate for young children. However, it is certainly an exceptional artistic achievement, and one that reflects the words attributed to Paula Rego that Janssen quotes on her website: 'I've never understood why "illustration" is used dismissively in the art world. To dismiss them [the illustrations from *Dante's Inferno* by Doré] because they are in a book is ridiculous. It's that stupid old "fine art" snobbery again.'

Jacob und Wilhelm Grimm / Susanne Janssen
Hänsel und Gretel

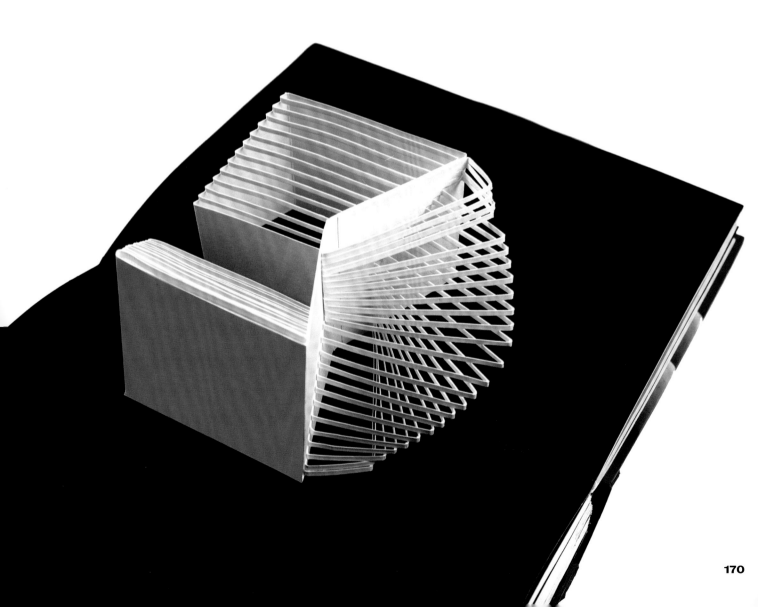

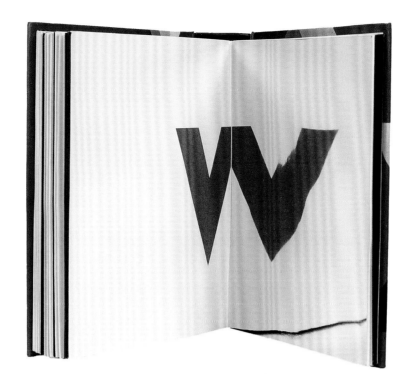

Bataille playfully toys with the visual relationship between alphabetically consecutive letters.

When neatly closed, the book's 3D secrets are completely hidden.

Marion Bataille
Published by Albin Michel
Jeunesse, Paris, 2008
This copy: 1st UK edition
(Bloomsbury, London, 2008)
185 x 140 x 40 mm
(7¼ x 5½ x 1½ in)

The illustrator and graphic artist Marion Bataille was born in 1963, and lives and works in Paris. As well as being an innovator in the design of pop-up books, she works for the Centre Pompidou and has created illustrations for many leading publications in France.

ABC 3D took the picturebook world by storm when it appeared in 2008. Within the industry, 3D or pop-up books tend to be saddled with the label 'novelty'; Bataille's books are much more than that. They straddle the worlds of picturebooks, *livres d'artistes* and toys. The artist has created a book-work whose paper engineering is never more complex than it needs to be, and yet is full of sequential twists and surprises. This is an ABC book that reads elegantly and fluently in pop-up form, with links made between letters, such as a mirror to turn a 'V' into a 'W'.

Using only red and black in addition to the white of the page, as well as an occasional use of reflective and transparent surfaces, Bataille takes us on a journey through the alphabet that feels akin to walking through a sculpture park. The book also closes neatly into a compact, pleasingly hand-sized form. This masterpiece of 3D design is published all over the world.

早上起来，宝儿发现母亲脸色苍白、神情恍惚，
着急地问："娘，你怎么了？是不是病了？"
母亲张了张嘴巴，却什么也说不出来。

"是谁把娘害成了这个样子？我一定要抓住他！"
宝儿又心疼又着急。
天亮后，宝儿用砖块和石灰把窗子封得严严实实，
又找来一把刀，在石头上磨得雪亮。

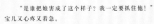

天黑时分，宝儿等母亲睡下了，悄悄抱着刀守到门
外，蹲了很久都没有动静，正要迷迷糊糊睡着的时候，
房间里又传来奇怪的哭闹声。
宝儿赶紧堵住门大叫起来。突然——

很久以前，在一座老宅子里，住着宝儿和他的父母。

宝儿的父亲是一个商人，经常外出做生意。这一天，
他又出远门了。
半夜里——

Full-bleed pages are
elegantly juxtaposed
with vignette illustrations
on white.

82
Bao'er (The boy who outfoxed a fox)

Xin Yi, illustrated by Cai Gao
Published by Hsin Yi Publication,
Taiwan, 2008
This copy: 1st edition
265 x 195 mm (10½ x 7¾ in)

Cai Gao was born in 1946 in
Changsha, in central southern
China. In 1993, her *Lonely Ghost
in the Abandoned Garden* won
the Golden Apple Award at the
Biennial of Illustrations Bratislava.
Her books have been published
in Japan and South Korea,
and in 2008 a major retrospective
of her work was exhibited at
Beihang University in Beijing,
along with a published book of her
collected works.

Of the new wave of Chinese
artists who work in the field
of picturebooks, Cai Gao stands
out for her mature fusion of rich
Chinese folk art and elements of
Western painting. *Bao'er* tells the
story of a boy who awakes one
night to find his mother in a state
of madness. He goes on a quest
to root out the source of the evil
fox spirits that have brought about
her condition. This is explored
through painterly artwork of rare
depth. The artist combines pattern
and space with unusual mastery
and an exceptional, vibrant use
of complementary colours – in
particular, reds and greens – set
against black.

As the picturebook emerges
in China as an art form, rather
than a purely didactic medium,
the magnificent artwork of Cai
Gao will provide a solid foundation.

这天晚上，宝儿家出奇的平静，母亲睡得安稳极了。

天亮后，宝儿带着父亲来到荒园，一进去，就看见
三只狐狸直挺挺地倒在地上，已经没有了气息，再仔细
一看，其中有一只狐狸的尾巴果然断了一截。

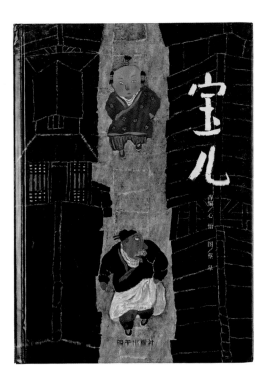

Cai Gao's striking use of
reds and greens against black
gives the page great depth.

Each story opens with
a beautifully designed,
coarsely executed
patterned title page.

Atak's illustrations make reference to Dr Heinrich Hoffmann's original *Struwwelpeter* while bringing a primitive yet modern 'punk' dynamic to the page.

83
Pierre-Crignasse

Fil & Atak
Published by Kein & Aber Verlag, Zurich/Berlin, 2009
This copy: 1st French-language edition (Frémok, Brussels, 2011)
270 x 210 mm (10½ x 8¼ in)

Georg Barber, aka Atak, grew up in East Berlin, where he made his name in the avant-garde comic scene by founding the subversive magazine *Renate*. He studied visual communication at Berlin's University of the Arts, where he later returned to teach, in addition to holding temporary posts as a professor of illustration at several other institutions. He is currently Chair of Illustration at Giebichenstein University of Art and Design, in Halle. In recent years Atak has also engaged with the art of picturebook making.

Heinrich Hoffmann's seminal collection of cautionary tales, *Der Struwwelpeter* (Shock-headed Peter), first appeared in 1845. To mark the 200th anniversary of Hoffmann's birth, Atak created this lavishly produced version of the original, in collaboration with Fil who updated the text. (Fil and Atak's 2009 edition was published in German with the same title as the original.) Fil's text displays an even harsher morality than Hoffmann's original, and Atak's illustrations give us a suitably raw, uncompromising visual interpretation.

One of the more notable aspects of Atak's work is his ability to combine an apparently crude, primitive approach to drawing and composition with a highly sophisticated flair for colour and visual narration. The Franco-Belgian publishing house Frémok, which produced the edition pictured here, specializes in publishing challenging and unorthodox books and comics.

A single colour, red, is used for this spread of character portraits. Cross-hatched cutting gives a half-tone texture to the background.

Where full-bleed images are used on a single page, they are usually offset by plenty of white on the facing page.

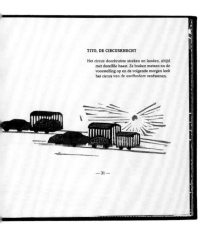

The cover boards are simply
bound in green canvas,
embossed with dramatic
red type and a single image.

84
**Het circus van Dottore
Fausto (The circus of
Doctor Faustus)**

Pieter van Oudheusden, illustrated
by Isabelle Vandenabeele
Published by De Eenhoorn,
Belgium, 2010
This copy: number 470 of a
hand-numbered edition of 750.
274 x 300 mm (10¾ x 11¾ in)

The excellent small publishing
house of De Eenhoorn in Flemish
Belgium has been responsible
for a number of highly imaginative
and influential picturebooks.
A culture of the picturebook as
a key sector of the arts prevails
in this region of Belgium, and
support for the production of
such books as this one comes
from the Flemish Literature Fund.
This support allows for a level
of creativity and experiment that
is less easily achieved in the
mainstream English-language
publishing industry.

Het circus van Dottore Fausto
straddles the boundary between
picturebook and *livre d'artiste*. The
simple typographic cover features
red text on plain, green canvas-
covered boards. Vandenabeele's
characteristically raw, robust and
muscular woodcuts are executed in
just two colours, red and dark grey,
giving a third colour, a deep brown/
black, when the two are overlaid.
With such limitations the artist
ingeniously designs spreads that
create a fabulous, grotesque world
of mystery and intrigue.

Quella si vedeva che era appena spuntata
e non aveva nessuna intenzione di farsi staccare.
Al principio il bambino se l'era arrotolata in vita,
sperando che nessuno la notasse,
ma la coda era tutt'altro che docile,
s'imbizzarriva a essere costretta, **schioccava** contro le pareti.

The use of just red and black
against a textured, warm,
off-white background gives
the book a strong sense
of continuity.

la coda canterina

Guia Risari e Violeta Lopiz

Topipittori

Furono mobilitati, insomma,
uno dopo l'altro,
tutti gli abitanti del paese.
Era un paese tanto piccolo
che l'appello non durò molto.
Arrivò il becchino con le bare invisibili
e il tabaccaio con le sigarette tagliate a metà;
il fruttivendolo con una mela sì e due no
e il giornalaio che una pagina
la faceva durare settimane.

Per ultimo apparve il sindaco
con la sua tuba di cartone.
E propose: "Tiriamo".

**Text is sensitively integrated
into the pictorial whole.**

Il bambino, chiuso in bagno, cercò di affogarla,
ma la coda nell'acqua galleggiava, danzava;
provò pure a fare gargarismi,
sorgille e gilrni sempre giocorre.
e poiché i genitori del bambino accorsero.

"**Ivaan, Ivaan**", lo chiamarono e poiché in risposta
giungevano solo grida soffocate,
cominciarono a tempestare la porta di pugni
e alla fine la sfondarono.

Guia Risari, illustrated by
Violeta Lopiz
Published by Topipittori,
Milan, 2010
This copy: 1st edition
198 x 198 mm (7¾ x 7¾ in)

Milan-based independent
publishers Topipittori are
responsible for so many beautiful
books that we are spoilt for choice.
Here, writer and translator Guia
Risari gives us a story of a boy
who wakes up with a tail. Not just
any tail, however, but a singing tail.
And not just any singing tail but
one that sings in Russian and does
not stay still for a moment, to the
considerable consternation of the
boy's parents and the entire village.

This surreal concept is
beautifully realized in a stunningly
designed book. The string-like tail
runs wild throughout the book,
dancing with the text and creating
patterns that form a structure
for a totally integrated design.
Printed entirely in two colours –
red and various tones of black
– Lopiz's illustrations employ a
wide range of textures through
drawing and creating collage with
found material.

Lopiz was born in Ibiza but
moved to Madrid, where, she
says, she immersed herself in
illustration and music in order to
recall the lost sea and nature of
her island home. She has studied
with leading artists, such as Javier
Zabala, Linda Wolfsgruber and
Józef Wilkoń, but claims that her
own childhood has been one of
the biggest influences on her
work. Now based in Berlin, Lopiz
contributes illustrations to a range
of newspapers and magazines
around Europe alongside her
book work.

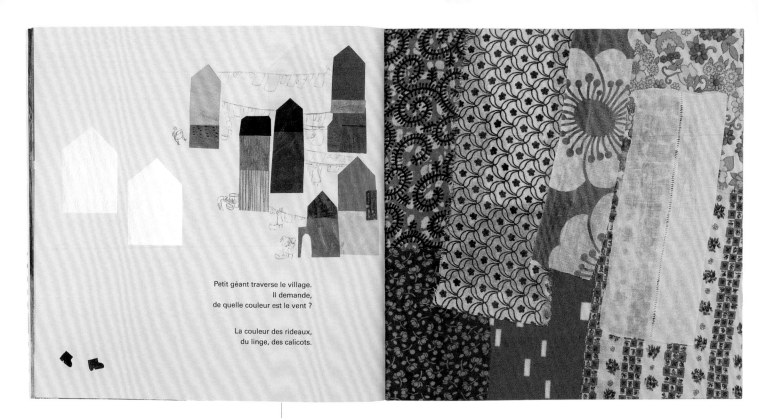

Petit géant traverse le village.
Il demande,
de quelle couleur est le vent ?

La couleur des rideaux,
du linge, des calicots.

A range of finishing
techniques, such as
embossing and varnishing,
creates surface textures
that can be explored by
one's fingertips as a form
of pictorial braille.

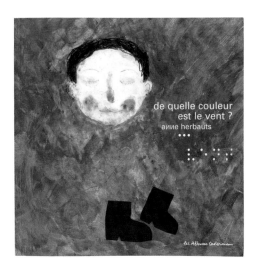

de quelle couleur
est le vent ?
anne herbauts

les Albums Casterman

When touched, tiny raised dots give the unsighted (and the sighted) the experience of raindrops.

86
De quelle couleur est le vent? (What colour is the wind?)

Anne Herbauts
Published by Casterman, Tournai, Belgium, 2010
This copy: 1st edition
249 x 249 x 70 mm
(9¾ x 9¾ x 2¾ in)

A blind child asks the question, 'What colour is the wind?' In this sensual picturebook, the Belgian artist Anne Herbauts takes the little boy on a quest to answer his own question. He encounters a dog, a mountain, a window and the rain. He questions them all, and his questions open up a world that makes sense to both the seeing and the sightless.

The book is produced with tactile elements to encourage touch. Embossed and varnished to give different textures to the surface of the page, it allows one to feel the silhouette of an elephant and to 'touch' the rain.

Herbauts was born in Belgium and graduated from the Royal Academy of Fine Arts in Brussels, where she studied comics and illustration under Anne Quévy and Bruno Goose. She has since returned to Brussels to teach at the same establishment. As well as creating numerous picturebooks, Herbauts also works on comics and visual texts for older audiences. Her books are always intellectually and artistically curious, and invariably beautiful.

Alors, il demande à la pluie,
de quelle couleur est le vent ?

Mais la pluie n'en sait rien.

Non, bleu,
souffle la montagne.

87

Jag-eun Dangnagwi
(Little donkey)

Yein Kim
Published by Nurimbo, Seoul, 2010
This copy: 2nd edition
225 x 240 mm (9 x 9½ in)

Yein (or 'Yanni') Kim is a New York-based Korean artist who won the CJ Picture Book Award in 2010 with this, her debut book. The story tells of a little donkey who dreams of escaping the daily routine of the city. One day, the donkey hears a travelling busker singing songs of a mysterious forest beyond the bustle of the city, where the air is pure and silent. The donkey goes in search of this place, but the townsfolk are suspicious and believe there are riches hidden there.

Telling her allegorical story with a masterful sense of space and delicately applied washes, Kim explores the treadmill of modern urban living. Occasional splashes of colour break out of the dominant urban greys to indicate life and hope.

First published in South Korea, the book is now also available in French, under the title *Petite Anette*. Published by the RMN-Grand Palais imprint, Collection Ramino, under the editorial direction of Beatrice Alemagna (see pages 165 and 185), it joins a list of picturebooks that are selected as *livres d'artistes pour la jeunesse* – artists' books for young people.

Kim uses brush, ink and pencil to create the monochrome world of the city dwellers, with the tiniest hint of warmth here and there on the page.

Alemagna's combination
of drawing and collage is
augmented by a new, raw
graphic edge that suits
its subject.

e-garçon.
t ce qu'il croyait
jeune âge.

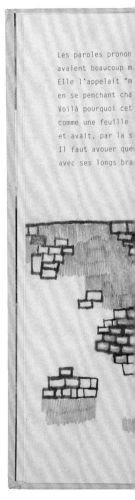

Les paroles pronon
avaient beaucoup m
Elle l'appelait "m
en se penchant cha
Voilà pourquoi cet
comme une feuille
et avait, par la s
Il faut avouer que
avec ses longs bra

Un jour,
un enfant partit
vivre au zoo.

Jo singe garçon

Jo
singe
garçon

Beatrice Alemagna

au-dessus du berceau

babouin, mon-sapajou".

embrasser.

glissée dans sa tête

pe ouverte

ensée et ses gestes.

un garçon fort joli,

hirsutes.

88
Jo singe garçon
(Jo monkey boy)

Beatrice Alemagna
Published by Autrement Jeunesse,
Paris, 2010
This copy: 1st edition
275 x 215 mm (10¾ x 8½ in)

Alemagna's constant urge to experiment – graphically and conceptually – takes her into ever-changing territories on the borders between commercial art and the book arts. In this work from 2010 she tells the story of a boy who lives like a monkey. He swings from trees, eats with his hands, sleeps balancing in strange places, and attentively grooms the hair of others. In despair, his parents send him to see a psychiatrist. Eventually, he decides to go and live with his soulmates, the monkeys at the zoo.

In *Jo singe garçon*, Alemagna poetically explores the world of a small boy and his growing self-awareness. She draws with a range of media and combines this with limited use of photographic collage. And there is a raw edge to her drawing, which more fully evokes her subject matter. There are hints of new graphic influences too, such as the work of Ben Shahn (see page 83), but these are always absorbed into her own personal visual language, never overt.

The production of this book also subtly reflects its content. The cover boards and internal pages are a buff, everyday, uncoated brown, further evoking the visceral aspects of the book and making it a particular pleasure to hold and feel. And at 64 pages, the book breaks out of the standard 32-page mould, giving us an extended gallery of this important artist's work.

The hand-rendered title on the brown cover boards adds to the 'rough and ready' aesthetic.

うさぎくんと
はるちゃん

おかだちあき さく・え

おかだこう さく

〜とりで、 ほかのおもちゃにも ほうたい まいた。
〜るちゃんは、 みんなに えほんを よんでくれた。

Okada's sensitive use of
naturalistic lighting gives
extra resonance to this
image of the 'standoff'
between the two characters.

89

Usagi-kun to Haru-chan
(Master Rabbit and
Miss Haru)

Ko Okada, illustrated by
Chiaki Okada
Published by Iwasaki Publishing
Co., Tokyo, 2010
This copy: 1st edition
265 x 215 mm (10½ x 8½ in)

The gentle, quiet world of Chiaki
Okada's illustrations first caught
the eye of the West at the 2010
Bologna Children's Book Fair,
her series of subtly lit interior and
exterior landscapes standing out for
its narrative power. *Master Rabbit
and Miss Haru* (this is a suggested
translation, as the book has not
yet been published in English)
tells the story of a sleepover, where
the visitor is less happy about
leaving home than his host is about
receiving him. Gradually, the ice is
broken as Miss Haru repairs Master
Rabbit's broken toy. The text was
written by Okada's husband, Ko.

It is Okada's exceptional
draughtsmanship and deep
understanding of light that make
this book special. The fall of light
across bedclothes somehow
heightens the contrast between
the two characters' states of
mind. And the sickly yellow glow
of morning light emphasizes
Master Rabbit's loneliness as he
comes down for breakfast. Okada
uses a painstaking process that
begins with traditional tonal pencil
drawing but then proceeds through
scanning and printing on to slightly
textured paper and applying colour
to the prints. Unusually, light is
described partly through the pencil
rendering and partly by careful use
of the white of the paper, which
is allowed occasionally to peep
through the washes of colour.
This book has been published in
numerous languages, including
Spanish, Russian and French (*Ma
première nuit ailleurs*, or My First
Night Elsewhere).

はじめての よるは しらないおとが
いっぱい きこえる。
わにくんだけは いつものにおい。
ぼくの おうちのにおい、あったかい。

しずかな しずかな
あさの かいだん。
そーっと
おとを たてないように。

とおくで だれかが、じてんしゃを こぐ おとがする。
おかあさん、ぐあいは どうかな。

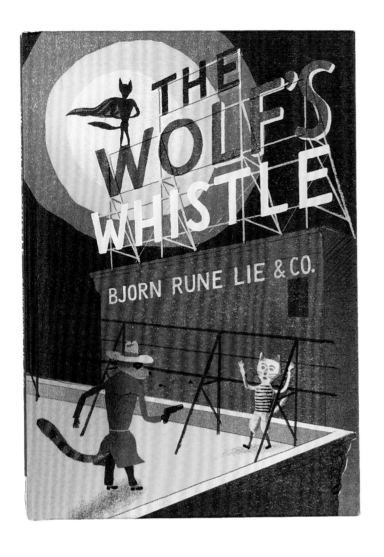

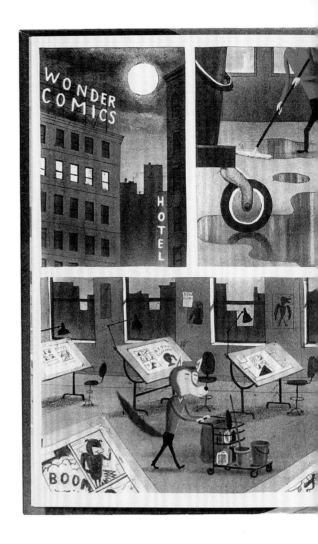

Once upon a time there was a wolf-cub named Albert. He lived with his dad, a salty sea-dog, in a small, crumbling house down by the docks. They were poor, they could barely rub two pennies together, but still every Saturday Albert's dad gave him a shiny coin to take with him to his favourite comic book store.

Using limited 'spot' colour
separations on uncoated
paper, Lie creates a world
of mid-twentieth-century
cheap Americana.

Endpapers using textured
separations of blue and red
set the scene.

90
The Wolf's Whistle

Bjørn Rune Lie
Published by Nobrow,
London, 2010
This copy: 1st edition
208 x 155 mm (8¼ x 6 in)

The London-based independent
company Nobrow has, in the
few short years of its existence,
established itself as a highly
innovative and influential presence
on the publishing scene. For those
with an interest in books that are
concerned with the visual, a visit
to its shop and gallery in London's
Shoreditch is a must.

Norwegian artist Bjørn Rune
Lie studied illustration at University
College Falmouth and now lives in
Bristol. As well as creating award-
winning picturebooks, he works
across a range of design contexts,
illustrating for such leading
publications as the *New York
Times* and creating pattern designs
for furnishing, bags and textiles.
Clients include Kauniste of Finland
and Aristu in Barcelona.

The Wolf's Whistle sits
somewhere between the
picturebook and the graphic
novel, and tells the story of the
Three Little Pigs and the Big
Bad Wolf from a slightly different
perspective. Lie creates a faux
comic/film noir detective story set
in the pulp fiction world of 1940s
urban America. In his own words:
'*The Wolf's Whistle* tells the rather
sad story of what could have
happened before the well-known
fairy tale of the *Three Little Pigs*.
Pehaps "The Big Bad Wolf" had a
perfectly good reason for blowing
down those houses? Perhaps he
wasn't such a nasty character after
all? The book is lovingly printed in
three spot colours, red, yellow and
blue (a little tip of the hat to Theo
van Doesburg).'

Negrin creates intense panoramic compositions that could easily be envisioned as murals.

À la fête des Morts, une grande veillée est célébrée
au cimetière. On apporte des offrandes aux défunts et,
durant toute la nuit, le cimetière se remplit de monde,
de musique et de lumières.
Frida et sa famille s'installent entre la tombe du grand-père
et celle d'une vieille tante. En quelques minutes,
ils les recouvrent de dizaines de bougies. Sur des morceaux
de tissus rouges, ils disposent de façon géométrique
les plats préférés des défunts et, tout autour, des vases
débordant de fleurs jaune orangé : les *cempasúchil*,
les roses d'Inde, réservées à cette fête. Les deux morts
seront tellement contents !

Frida sort les petits crânes en sucre de son panier et
les empile sur la tombe de son grand-père. Alors qu'elle
relève la tête pour admirer la pyramide de friandises,
elle voit Diego à quelques pas d'elle, à moitié caché
dans les buissons.

A clever use of cutaway
illustrations augments the
dream-world atmosphere.

91

Frida et Diego: au pays des squelettes (Frida and Diego in the land of skeletons)

Fabian Negrin
Published by Seuil Jeunesse,
Paris, 2011
This copy: 1st edition
352 x 260 mm (14 x 10¼ in)

Negrin was born in Argentina,
but is now based in Italy, where he
has lived for more than 20 years.
He is one of the most prolific and
versatile artists working in the field
of picturebooks today. Despite
being seen as something of a
chameleon, owing to the many and
varied stylistic ways in which he
approaches projects, there is an
unmistakable graphic language that
underpins all of his work.

  Frida et Diego is a tour de force.
The very large scale of the book
does full justice to the extraordinary
artworks that accompany this
imaginary story of the Mexican
artists Frida Kahlo and Diego Rivera
as children, celebrating the Day
of the Dead. The macabre subject
matter is brought to life through
rich Mexican colours and motifs,
and a masterful use of watercolour.
Negrin realizes highly imaginative,
dreamlike constructions with
rare technical skill to create an
astonishingly beautiful book. There
are references to primitivist artists
– Rousseau and Gauguin, for
instance – but these are subsumed
into a language of more naturalistic
space and lighting.

  At the end of this spectacular
visual journey, we are given some
key facts about Kahlo, Diego and
other key players.

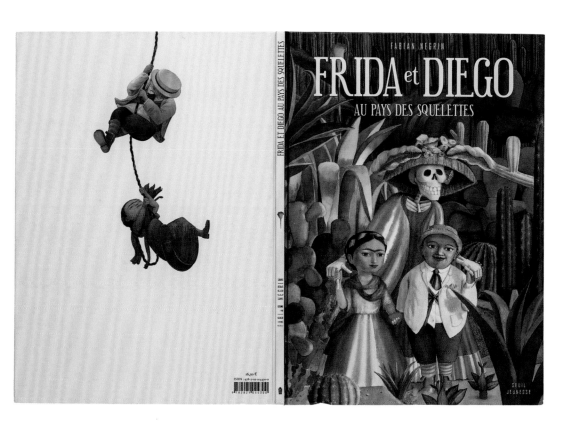

Klassen uses simplified, flattened shapes and minute changes in the bear's expressions to convey the narrative in a highly subtle manner.

I WANT MY HAT BACK

JON KLASSEN

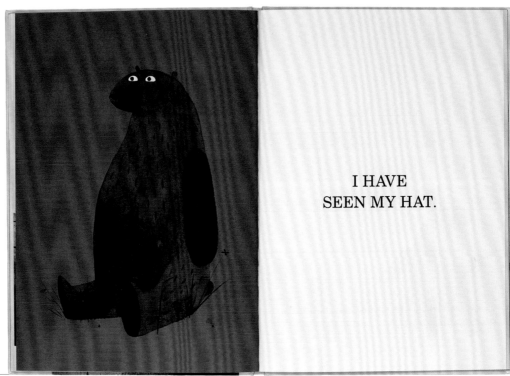

I HAVE
SEEN MY HAT.

The colour red and uppercase type are used sparingly for maximum impact.

Jon Klassen
Published by Walker Books,
London, 2011
This copy: 1st edition
285 x 205 mm (11¼ x 8 in)

Having graduated in animation
from Sheridan College in his native
Canada in 2005, Klassen moved
to Los Angeles, where he worked
on the films *Kung Fu Panda* (2008)
and *Coraline* (2009). Described by
Pamela Paul in her *New York Times*
review as a 'charmingly wicked little
book', this was Klassen's debut as
a picturebook maker. It would not
be an overstatement to describe
this groundbreaking book as
something of a game-changer for
the industry. It breaks all the usual
rules of redemption and happy
endings and gets away with it, due
to its brilliant minimalist humour and
respect for its reader.

Klassen fully exploits the linear
form of the picturebook as we
follow an expressionless bear on
his left-to-right journey through the
pages of the book in search of his
lost hat. All matters that are not
hat-related are depicted in shades
of brown; the one other colour –
red – appears only in relation to
the missing hat. The tiniest changes
in the depiction of the bear's
eyes assume massive narrative
power, indicating his moments of
realization. It is at these moments
that the bear heads back in the
other direction to solve the mystery.

The book is a masterpiece of
seamlessly integrated narrative
design and typography. Everything
is pared down to the bare
essentials; nothing appears on the
page unless it contributes to the
narrative structure.

Have you seen my hat?

No. Why are you asking me.
I haven't seen it.
I haven't seen any hats anywhere.
I would not steal a hat.
Don't ask me any more questions.

OK. Thank you anyway.

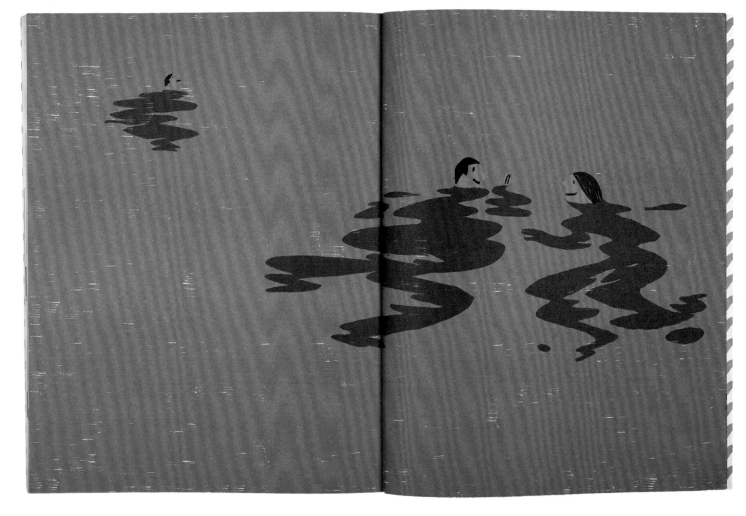

Shapes and colours hover
and only occasionally hint
at space or perspective.

The white of the paper is
revealed only in small areas,
giving the impression of an
extra 'colour'.

93
Praia mar (High tide)

Bernardo Carvalho
Published by Planeta Tangerina,
Carcavelos, Portugal, 2011
This copy: 1st edition
350 x 270 mm (13¾ x 10½ in)

The Portuguese independent
publishing house Planeta Tangerina
is one of the most innovative and
influential to have emerged in
recent years. Its picturebooks are
being noticed all over the world,
and are beginning to appear in
ever more languages. Describing
its approach to publishing, the
company says: 'Our readers are not
only children, but all parents and
adults who enjoy picturebooks and
their unique way of telling a story.
We know that our books are not
always the "easiest" to read, but
we like to think that a picturebook
is a meeting point for readers of
different kinds, that some will open
doors for others, that big and small
readers will find their own keys to
the discovery of a book.'
   Praia mar is a very large-format,
flat-colour pictorial narrative. To
quote the publisher again: 'There
are no words on the pages and
readers, who are used to the
presence of a text that leads them
by the hand, may feel rather lost …'
   The book began life as a home-
printed edition of ten screen-
printed books for family and friends,
with a personal introduction by
Carvalho, explaining his relationship
with the beach and the sea.
The published edition is offset
litho, but it retains a handmade
feel. Printed in just four colours
throughout, created as separations
in the manner of screen-printing, it
celebrates the shapes and colours
that people and things make
on the beach and in the water,
and displays Carvalho's usual
fascination with people and their
everyday lives. Carvalho is the co-
founder with Isabel Minhós Martins
of Planeta Tangerina.

Il va au poulailler, de ses petits pas sans bruit,
et les poules caquètent de joie quand il arrive.
Il leur parle à la manière du lutin, une petite langue
silencieuse que les poules peuvent comprendre.

Pondez-moi un œuf, mes poulettes,
Et je vous donnerai du grain à manger.

La neige blanche s'entasse sur la niche du chien, c'est ici
qu'habite Karo. Il attend, il attend chaque nuit le moment
où le lutin va passer. Le lutin est son ami le plus cher,
il parle à Karo à la manière du lutin, une petite langue
silencieuse qu'un chien peut comprendre.

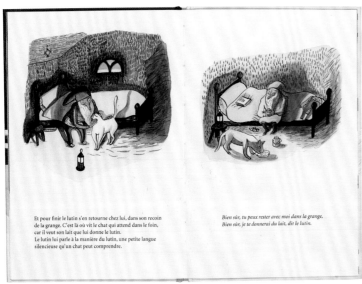

Et pour finir le lutin s'en retourne chez lui, dans son recoin
de la grange. C'est là où vit le chat qui attend dans le foin,
car il veut son lait que lui donne le lutin.
Le lutin lui parle à la manière du lutin, une petite langue
silencieuse qu'un chat peut comprendre.

Bien sûr, tu peux rester avec moi dans la grange,
Bien sûr, je te donnerai du lait, dit le lutin.

Crowther creates a silent, snowy night-time world with heavy brushstrokes of opaque white paint over a pale yellow base.

Astrid Lindgren & Kitty Crowther

LUTIN VEILLE

Pastel

C'est une de ces nuits où les gens se recroquevillent dans leurs petites maisons et ne laissent pas le feu s'éteindre dans l'âtre. Ici se dresse une vieille ferme où tout le monde dort. Tout le monde, sauf un…

Les hivers viennent et les étés s'en vont, mais tant que des hommes habiteront la vieille ferme dans la forêt, le lutin fera son va-et-vient à petits pas feutrés, la nuit, entre les bâtiments.

Lutin veille (Elf eve)

Astrid Lindgren, illustrated by
Kitty Crowther
Published by L'École des Loisirs,
Paris, 2012
This copy: 1st edition
265 x 180 mm (10½ x 7 in)

The importance of this wonderful artist to the world of children's picturebooks was underlined by her receipt of the Astrid Lindgren Memorial Award in 2010 – the highest honour in the field of children's literature. Born in Belgium in 1970 to a British father and a Swedish mother, Crowther has already generated a substantial body of award-winning work as a picturebook maker. Writing about her inspirations and motivations after receiving the award, she said: 'From the outset, I have always been completely captivated by stories of all kinds. They develop you internally, they fine-tune your senses. They are like an act of breathing: in, out; in, out. Some people have an irrepressible urge to go out walking. But I had this irrepressible urge to walk inside my own head.'

And on the subject of her art: 'There are so many different forms and levels of art, and what point is there in saying that this is good and this is not? I am often impressed by people who have a visceral love of things that contrast with the things I love. But is not that all of the richness of human existence? It is sad that art is becoming entangled in a kind of snobbery.'

Lutin veille brings Crowther and Lindgren together in the latter's gentle story of a silent, unseen old elf (a Swedish *tomte*, or house spirit, associated with Christmas). He passes through the snowy night, talking to the animals and dreaming of warmer days.

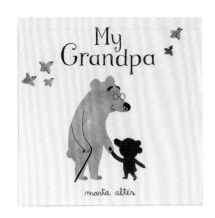

Just two basic colours are used in order to isolate key shapes and to direct the eye across the spreads.

Some days,
I am his eyes …

Sometimes he feels alone.

Together we have travelled the world . . .

Reality and fantasy are
combined seamlessly
through the use of shapes
as 'props' and the absence
of background.

Marta Altés
Published by Macmillan Children's
Books, London, 2012
This copy: 1st edition
225 x 225 mm (9 x 9 in)

Having trained and worked as a
graphic designer in Barcelona for
several years, Altés then moved
to the UK, where she took an MA
in Children's Book Illustration at
Cambridge School of Art. She now
teaches on the same course. Altés
shot to prominence with her debut
book, *No!*, which was published
by Child's Play in 2011. It won
numerous awards for innovative
artwork and humorous interplay
between word and image, telling
the story of a naughty but well-
meaning dog. In this, her second
picturebook, she demonstrates her
versatility with a complete change
of tone. *My Grandpa* deals with
ageing and the onset of dementia.
It does so through the sensitive
portrayal of the relationship
between a child and a grandparent,
as experienced and told by
the child.

The issue of memory loss is
never explicit, but is handled with
empathy, elegance and a lightness
of touch, embodying Maurice
Sendak's use of the term 'visual
poem' to describe the essence
of a successful picturebook.
The complex relationship between
grandparent and child is handled
gently, without sentimentality, using
minimal shapes in two colours plus
a graphite pencil line against the
white of the page.

Altés has a profound
understanding of the relationship
between word and image in a
picturebook, and how this can
be exploited. She is able to create
silence, space, movement and
drama through her command of the
grammar and metre of the medium.

So they sang, these two in their speed trances. Through the centuries John became a little old man with white hair and Raven became a little old Raven whose white feathers were starting to fall out. They sang themselves hoarse, they sang until John lost his voice and Raven could only croak.

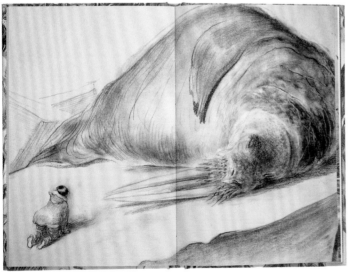

Text is reversed out of the image, using the white of the underlying paper and echoing the facing light on the figures.

After fifte
John said to
hear somethi
They both
something.
They liste
down the tu
towards them
through the
more and the
Song that co
in John's ha
into his mout

The sepia image used on
the cover boards gives
a sense of both narrative
and decorative pattern.

96
Soonchild

Russell Hoban, illustrated by
Alexis Deacon
Published by Walker Books,
London, 2012
This copy: 1st edition
236 x 160 mm (9¼ x 6¼ in)

Hoban's last book before his death
in 2011 does not sit comfortably
in the category of picturebook,
or in any other labelled box for
that matter. The author's richly
imaginative text is, however,
spectacularly and generously
accompanied by Alexi Deacon's
exquisite draughtsmanship.

A close working relationship
between Deacon and the designer
Ben Norland was key to the
visual quality of this book. Deacon
selected passages of text that
he wished to illustrate, and the
two of them agreed the amount
of space required for each. The
pencil drawings are accompanied
by Deacon's simple hand-rendered
chapter-heading text and front-
cover titling – also in pencil.

The production of the book
is carefully considered, too.
Differently coloured papers are
used as backdrops to the artist's
pencil drawings. Both Deacon
and Norland felt that these pale
background colours gave the
book a stronger overall sense of
visual progression. But it is the
sheer force of imagination and
storytelling skill – of writer and
artist – that makes this such an
exceptional book.

Deacon studied illustration
at the University of Brighton,
graduating in 2001. His book
Beegu was nominated for the Kate
Greenaway Medal in 2004, and he
was named as one of Booktrust's
Best New Illustrators in 2008.
Not since Mervyn Peake has there
been a British illustrator of such
unique vision.

The extreme portrait format of the page makes a suitable frame for this visual journey up and up a fantasy fusion of cactus and dwelling.

As with all the books from this small South Korean enterprise, great care is taken with every aspect of *The Thorn Mountain*'s production. Each copy is carefully hand-wrapped in tissue paper.

97
The Thorn Mountain

Park Sunmi
Published by Some Books/
Sunkyung Cho, Seoul, 2012
This copy: number 499 in an
edition of 585
241 x 150 mm (9½ x 6 in)

The artist and teacher Sunkyung Cho set up his small publishing house, Some Books, in 2007 with the mission to publish picturebooks that are not driven by commercial interests. The books are typically produced with simple, coarse card covers and limited colour on well-chosen paper stock. They are beautifully printed, often handmade, and yet affordable.

Many of these books are the work of graduates of the Some Institute of Picturebooks (SI), which Sunkyung Cho founded and leads. Park Sunmi completed her course at SI in 2011, and this is her first picturebook.

The Thorn Mountain is in the form of a continuous linear visual journey that carries its reader upwards, climbing the length of a giant cactus, densely rendered in black ink. As we climb the cactus, we discover elements of cityscape and shantytown subtly emerging from its skin, until the top of the cactus is revealed in a final single burst of colour. The book was one of two to receive a prestigious 'special mention' in the Opera Prima category (awarded for a debut book) of the 2013 Bologna Ragazzi Awards. The jury's statement enthused: 'Clinging to one of the most ancient symbols, a living plant, this world of dark colours and lines, its sombre horizons narrowly confined, seems inhabited by hidden presences. A very modern metaphor is here deployed with the rhythm of an ancient fable, giving form to very real childhood anxieties. For as we climb the vertical city we do not know whether we will find a flower at the top.'

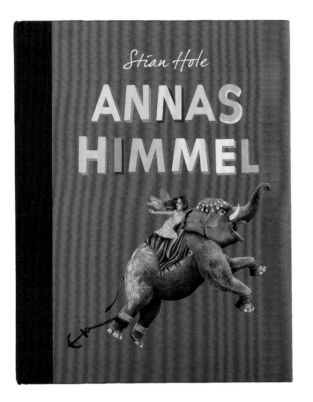

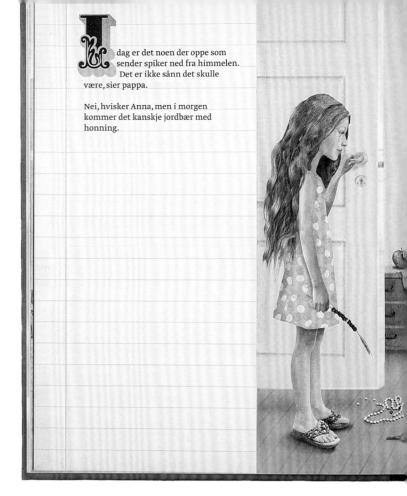

dag er det noen der oppe som sender spiker ned fra himmelen. Det er ikke sånn det skulle være, sier pappa.

Nei, hvisker Anna, men i morgen kommer det kanskje jordbær med honning.

Det hender at noen brev forsvinner på veien, svarer pappa.

Stian Hole
Published by Cappelen Damm,
Oslo, 2013
This copy: 1st edition
275 x 215 mm (10¾ x 8½ in)

Many Scandinavian picturebooks are labelled 'all age books'; such books as *Annas himmel* do not talk down to the reader and can be appreciated on different levels by readers of all ages. Its Norwegian author and illustrator, Stian Hole, came to wider prominence when his *Garmann's sommer* won the Ragazzi Award in the fiction category at the 2010 Bologna Children's Book Fair. That book has since been translated into numerous languages, including English, and the character of Garmann now has his own series of books, which follows him as he grows up.

Hole constructs his illustrations as layered digital montages in Photoshop. He amasses images and textures, then scans, sketches and works in an intense, painterly and extremely time-consuming manner, reassembling and manipulating his material, and taking total control of all aspects of the image-making process. It is only in recent years that Hole's work has at last begun to reach a wider audience, and the stunning *Annas himmel* has already been sold to publishers in the US and elsewhere.

The book tells the moving story of Anna, who tries to comfort her father on the day of her mother's funeral. Hole's work reaches new heights of emotional intensity in a visual rollercoaster that requires many hours of 'reading'. The book is beautifully produced, with attention having been given to every aspect of its physical form.

Hole's output, and that of many other Norwegian book artists, owes much to the visionary editor Ellen Seip at Cappelen Damm, who has overseen the publication of many important picturebooks from this part of the world.

Hole's painterly use of photo manipulation is carefully colour controlled, producing a powerful and disturbingly intense image.

le had grown as mean and hard and ugly as their city,

and I was mean and hard and ugly too.

I lived by stealing from those who had almost as little as I did.

My heart was as shrivelled as the dead trees in the park.

Nothing grew.   Everything was broken.   No one ever smiled.

*I ran off without a backward look,
thinking of the food and money in her bag.*

and another ...

Carlin's intense exploration of the patterns of urban landscapes adds texture to the page.

A narrative wrap-around dust-jacket design with hand-rendered titling and no external blurb covers a separate motif on the printed cover boards.

99
The Promise

Nicola Davies, illustrated by
Laura Carlin
Published by Walker Books,
London, 2013
This copy: 1st edition
255 x 265 mm (10 x 10½ in)

In *The Promise*, Nicola Davies tells a tale of dark urban malice, relieved by a promise to plant a tree – a promise that is passed on, and on. Laura Carlin's superb draughtsmanship has graced a number of books for older readers, including the impressive Walker Books edition of Ted Hughes's *The Iron Man* (2010), which received an honourable mention in the Bologna Ragazzi Awards fiction category. This is Carlin's first picturebook.

The artist revels in the space to tell a complete story in pictures; her familiar fascination with the textures and patterns of the urban landscape is given free rein in the first half of the book. As the story unfolds, the dark inner-city colours give way to the green shoots and increasingly vivid colours of hope and growth. The endpapers combine these decorative patterns with what academics in the field of children's literature increasingly refer to as 'peritext' – the use of the peripheral, non-textual areas of a book to contribute to the narrative. Here, they are used to emphasize through colour and pattern the different moods at each end of the book.

Carlin studied at the Royal College of Art in London. During her time as a student there she won a number of awards, including the Sheila Robinson Prize for Drawing. As well as creating illustrations for books and magazines, Carlin works in 3D, making hand-painted ceramic pieces. She was also part of a team selected by Sir Quentin Blake to help set up his House of Illustration museum and archive in London's Kings Cross that opened in 2014.

The intensity of the flat colours means that shapes have to be carefully balanced across the page.

The dust jacket is printed on uncoated paper, enhancing the screen-print aesthetic of the imagery.

Goodnight
everyone!

Katherina Manolessou
Published by Macmillan Children's
Books, London, 2014
This copy: 1st edition
255 x 255 mm (10 x 10 in)

Originally from Greece,
Manolessou studied chemistry in
her home country before becoming
involved in animation and moving
to the UK to study illustration at
Kingston University and the Royal
College of Art. She has also
successfully completed a PhD
at Cambridge School of Art.

This stunning picturebook
formed part of the outcome
of her research into animal
characterization in children's
picturebooks. As a successful
illustrator in editorial and
advertising design, Manolessou
had always used animal characters
in her work, but she had never
attempted a children's picturebook
prior to her research project.
Printmaking has always been
central to her work – she is
a member of the East London
Printmakers collective – and *Zoom
Zoom Zoom* was developed entirely
using the screen-printing process.

The book is based on the rhyme
that many parents and young
children will be familiar with from
nursery school:
Zoom zoom zoom
We're going to the moon
Zoom zoom zoom
We'll be there very soon
Children chant the words together
before beginning a countdown-
5-4-3-2-1 ... Blast off!

Here, the rhyme is cleverly
adapted to include Monkey
and Bird – two characters who
cannot get to sleep, so zoom
off to the Moon for an adventure
before returning suitably sleepy.
Manolessou's unique visual
language brings intense areas
of flat colour to the page, and
bestows her characters with
warmth and empathy.

The Future

As with all areas of creative endeavour, the art of picturebook making continues to attract new talent, and new ideas and methods. Students in art schools are finding increasingly imaginative ways to experiment with the form, as the printed book continues to redefine its own unique territory alongside the burgeoning world of electronic publishing. Inevitably, it can take time for any invention and innovation on the boundaries of the discipline to be absorbed into the commercial publishing world. At the same time, the very best work usually comes from a mixture of respect for history and a healthy disrespect for convention. Academic research into the picturebook and its unique form of visual grammar continues to expand, straddling the fields of children's literature and art and design.

The examples of new works on these two pages, all at the time of writing unpublished (although each of the artists are now working with publishers on these and other concepts), are just a tiny sample of the many new creations being presented to the publishing world at any one time. It is, of course, impossible to predict where the next 'enduring classic' will come from. What we can say, though, is that the works on this page, along with many others, exhibit the highest standards of graphic, creative ambition.

Simona Ciraolo's unpublished dummy book, 'Whatever Happened To My Sister', explores a small child's bemusement at the changing interests and priorities of her older sibling. It does so with extreme sensitivity and graphic charm.

Mike Mason's work sits somewhere between book and toy. He is fascinated by the tensions and interplay between the two.

Becky Palmer is both an illustrator and a researcher. In both roles, she is exploring the boundaries between the picturebook and the graphic novel.

210

Further Reading

Books

Alderson, B. *Sing a Song for Sixpence: The English Picture Book Tradition and Randolph Caldecott.* Cambridge: Cambridge University Press and the British Library, 1986.

Alderson, B. and F. de Marez Oyens. *Be Merry and Wise: Origins of Children's Book Publishing in England, 1650–1850.* London: The British Library, 2006.

Amoss, B. and E. Suben. *Writing and Illustrating Children's Books for Publication: Two Perspectives.* Revised edition. Cincinnati: Writer's Digest Books, 2005.

Arizpe, E. and M. Styles. *Children Reading Pictures: Interpreting Visual Texts.* London: RoutledgeFalmer, 2003.

Backemeyer, S. (ed.). *Picture This: the Artist as Illustrator.* London: Central Saint Martins and Herbert Press, 2005.

Baddeley, P. and C. Eddershaw. *Not-so-simple Picture Books: Developing Responses to Literature with 4–12-Year-olds.* Stoke-on-Trent: Trentham Books, 1994.

Baines, P. *Puffin by Design: 70 Years of Imagination 1940–2010.* London: Allen Lane, 2010.

Barr, J. *Illustrated Children's Books.* London: The British Library, 1986.

Blake, Q. *Magic Pencil: Children's Book Illustration Today.* London: The British Library, 2002.

——. *Words and Pictures.* London: Jonathan Cape, 2000.

Bland, D. *A History of Book Illustration: The Illuminated Manuscript and the Printed Book.* London: Faber & Faber, 1958.

——. *The Illustration of Books.* London: Faber & Faber, 1953.

Brazell, D. and J. Davies. *Understanding Illustration.* London: Bloomsbury Visual Arts, 2014.

——. *Becoming a Successful Illustrator.* London: Fairchild Books, 2013

——. *The Making of Great Illustration.* London: A & C Black, 2011.

Chester, T. R. *Children's Book Research: A Practical Guide to Techniques and Sources.* Oxford: Thimble Press and Westminster College, 1989.

Children's Books: Special Issue. Graphis 155, 1972.

Children's Books: Special Issue. Graphis 177, 1976.

Colomer, T., B. Kümmerling and C. Silva-Diaz (eds) *New Directions in Picture Book Research.* London: Routledge, 2010.

Cummins, J. (ed.) *Children's Book Illustration and Design, Volume II.* Glen Cover, NY: PBC International, 1998.

Dalphin, M., B. Mahony Miller and R. H. Viguers. *Illustrators of Children's Books 1946–1956.* Boston: The Horn Book Co., 1972.

Doonan, J. *Looking at Pictures in Picture Books.* South Woodchester: Thimble Press, 1993.

Evans, D. *Show and Tell: Exploring the Fine Art of Children's Book Illustration.* San Francisco: Chronicle Books, 2008.

Evans, J. *What's in the Picture? Responding to Illustrations in Picture Books.* London: Paul Chapman, 1998.

Fisher, M. *Who's Who in Children's Books: a Treasury of the Familiar Characters of Childhood.* London: Weidenfeld and Nicolson, 1975.

Gauch, G. L., D. Briggs, and C. Palmer. *Artist to Artist: 23 Major Illustrators Talk About Their Art.* New York: Philomel Books, 2007.

Gibson, M. 'Picturebooks, comics and graphic novels' in D. Rudd (ed.) *The Routledge Companion to Children's Literature.* London: Routledge, 2010, pp. 100–111.

Graham, J. *Pictures on the Page.* Sheffield: National Association for the Teaching of English, 1990.

Harding, J. and P. Pinsent (eds). *What do You See? International Perspectives on Children's Book Illustration.* Cambridge: Cambridge Scholars Publishing, 2008.

Heller, S. and M. Arisman (eds). *The Education of an Illustrator.* New York: Allworth Press, 2000.

Horne, A. (ed.). *The Dictionary of Twentieth Century British Book Illustrators.* Woodbridge: Antique Collectors' Club, 1994.

Hunt, P., L. Sainsbury and D. McCorquodale. *Illustrated Children's Books.* London: Black Dog Publishing, 2009.

Hürlimann, B. *Three Centuries of Children's Books in Europe.* B. Alderson, trans. and ed. Oxford: Oxford University Press, 1968.

——. *Picture Book World.* B. Alderson, trans. and ed. Oxford: Oxford University Press, 1968.

Kiefer, B. Z. *The Potential of Picture Books: From Visual Literacy to Aesthetic Understanding.* Englewood Cliffs, N.J.: Merrill and Prentice Hall, 1995.

Kingman, L., J. Foster and R.G. Lontoft (eds) *Illustrators of Children's Books 1957–1966.* Boston: Horn Books, 1968.

Kingman, L. (ed.) *Newberry and Caldecott Medal Books 1966–1975.* Boston: Horn Books, 1975.

——. *The Illustrator's Notebook.* Boston: Horn Books, 1978.

——. *Newberry and Caldecott Medal Books 1976–1985.* Boston: Horn Books, 1987.

Klemin, D. The Art of Art for Children's Books: A Contemporary Survey. New York: Clarkson N. Potter, 1966.

——. *The Illustrated Book. Its Art and Craft.* New York: Clarkson N. Potter, 1970.

Kress, G. and T. Van Leeuwen. *Reading Images: The Grammar of Visual Design.* London: Routledge, 1996.

Lacy, L.E. *Art & Design in Children's Picture Books: An Analysis of Caldecott Award-winning Illustrations.* Chicago: American Library Association, 1986.

Lanes, S.G. *The Art of Maurice Sendak.* Vol. 1, revised edition. New York: Harry N. Abrams, 1998.

—— and T. Kushner. *The Art of Maurice Sendak: 1980 to the Present.* Vol. 2. New York: Harry N. Abrams, 2003.

——. *Through the Looking Glass: Further Adventures and Misadventures in the Realm of Children's Literature.* Boston: David R. Godine, 2004.

Lewis, D. *Reading Contemporary Picturebooks: Picturing Text.* London: RoutledgeFalmer, 2001.

Lewis, J. *The Twentieth Century Book: Its Illustration and Design.* London: The Herbert Press, 1984.

Marantz, S. and K.A. Marantz. *Artists of the Page: Interviews with Children's Book Illustrators.* Jefferson, N.C. and London: McFarland & Co., 1992.

——. *The Art of Children's Picture Books: a Selective Reference Guide.* 2nd edition. New York: Garland, 1995.

——. *Creating Picturebooks: Interviews with Editors, Art Directors, Reviewers, Professors, Librarians and Showcasers.* Jefferson, N.C. and London: McFarland & Co., 1997.

——. *Multicultural Picturebooks: Art for Illuminating Our World.* 2nd edition. Lanham, Md: Scarecrow Press, 2005.

Marcus, L.S. *Ways of Telling: Conversations on the Art of the Picture Book.* New York: Dutton Children's Books, 2002.

McCannon, D., S. Thornton and Y. Williams. *The Bloomsbury Guide to Creating Illustrated Children's Books.* London: A. & C. Black, 2008.

——. *The Encyclopedia of Writing and Illustrating Children's Books.* Philadelphia: Running Press, 2008.

Meek, M. *How Texts Teach What Readers Learn.* Stroud: Thimble Press, 1988.

Metaphors of Childhood. Catalogue of exhibition. Bologna: Editrice Compositiri, 2009.

Miller, B.M. and E.W. Field (eds). *Newberry Medal Books 1922–1955.* Boston: Horn Books, 1955.

Muir, P. *English Children's Books, 1600 to 1900.* London: B.T. Batsford, 1954.

Nikolajeva, M. and C. Scott. *How Picturebooks Work.* London: Routledge, 2006.

Noble, G., K. Rabey and Styles, M. *Picture This! Picture Book Art at the Millennium.* Cambridge: Fitzwilliam Museum, 2000.

Noble, I. and R. Bestley. *Visual Research: an Introduction to Research Methodologies in Graphic Design.* Lausanne: AVA, 2005.

Nodelman, P. *Words About Pictures: the Narrative Art of Children's Picture Books.* Athens, Ga. And London: University of Georgia Press, 1988.

Powers, A. *Children's Book Covers: Great Book Jacket and Cover Design.* London: Mitchell Beazley, 2003.

Salisbury, M. *Illustrating Children's Books: Creating Pictures for Publication.* London: A & C Black, 2004.

——. *Play Pen: New Children's Book Illustration.* London: Laurence King Publishing, 2007.

—— and M. Styles. *Children's Picturebooks: The art of visual storytelling.* London: Laurence King Publishing, 2012.

Schwarcz, J.H. *Ways of the Illustrator: Visual Communication in Children's Literature.* Chicago: American Library Association, 1982.

——and C. Schwarcz. *The Picture Book Comes of Age: Looking at Childhood through the Art of Illustration.* Chicago: American Library Association, 1991.

Sendak, M. *Caldecott & Co: Notes on Books and Pictures.* New York: Farrar, Strauss & Giroux, 1988.

Shulevitz, U. *Writing With Pictures: How to Write and Illustrate Children's Books.* New York: Watson-Guptill Publications, 1985.

Silvey, A. (ed.). *Children's Books and their Creators.* Boston: Houghton Mifflin, 1995.

Simon, F. (ed.). *The Children's Writers and Artists Year Book.* London: A & C Black, 2005–present.

Sipe, L. and S. Pantaleo (eds). *Postmodern Picturebooks: Play, Parody, and Self-Referentiality.* London: Routledge, 2008.

Spaulding, A.E. *The Page as a Stage Set: Story Board Picture Books.* London: Scarecrow Press, 1995.

Spitz, E.H. *Inside Picture Books.* New Haven: Yale University Press, 1999.

Steinev, E. *Stories for Little Comrades: Revolutionary Artists and the Making of Early Soviet Children's Books.* Seattle: University of Washington Press, 2000.

Styles, M. and E. Bearne (eds). *Art, Narrative and Childhood.* Stoke-on-Trent. Trentham Books, 2002.

Sutherland, Z. and M.H. Arbuthnot. *Children and Books. 8th edition.* New York: HarperCollins, 1991.

Trumpener, K. 'Picture-book worlds and ways of seeing'. *In M. Grenby and A. Immel (eds). The Cambridge Companion to Children's Literature.* Cambridge: Cambridge University Press, 2009, pp. 55–75.

Van der Linden, S. *Lire L'Album.* Le-Puy-en-Velay: L'Atelier du Poisson Soluble, 2006.

Vermeulen, M. *Colouring Outside the Lines: Flemish Illustrators Making Their Mark.* Antwerp: Flemish Literature Fund, 2003.

Watson, V. and M. Styles (eds). *Talking Pictures: Pictorial Texts and Young Readers.* London: Hodder & Stoughton, 1996.

Whalley, J.I. and T.R. Chester. *A History of Children's Book Illustration.* London: John Murray and Victoria and Albert Museum, 1988.

Wintle, J. and E. Fisher. *The Pied Pipers: Interviews with the Influential Creators of Children's Literature.* New York: Paddington Press, 1974.

Withrow, S. and L.B. Withrow. *Illustrating Children's Picture Books.* Hove: RotoVision, 2009.

Young, Timothy G. *Drawn to Enchant: Original Children's Book Art in the Betsy Beinbecke Shirley Collection.* New Haven and London: Yale University Press, 2007.

Periodicals

Bookbird
Children's Literature in Education
IRSCL online journal
The Lion and the Unicorn
New Review of Children's Literature and Librarianship
INIS
Books for Keeps online
Carousel
The Story of Picture Books (S. Korea)
The Bookseller

Websites

www.alma.se/en
www.anglia.ac.uk/ruskin/en/home/microsites/ccbs.html
www.associazioneillustratori.it
www.autrement.com
www.beatricealemagna.com
blaine.org/sevenimpossiblethings/
www.bolognafiere.it
www.bookbrunch.co.uk
www.booktrustchildrensbooks.org.uk/Picture-Books
www.carlemuseum.org
www.chihiro.jp
www.childrensillustrators.com
www.corraini.com
www.dibuixamunconte.blogspot.com
www.elblogdeilustrarte.blogspot.com
www.elblogdepencil.wordpress.com
www.houseofillustration.org.uk
www.ibby.org
www.ilustrarte.es
www.ilustrarte.net
www.itabashiartmuseum.jp
www.lefiguredeilibri.com
www.lerouergue.com
www.metm.co.jp
www.nccil.org/index.htm
www.orechioacerbo.com
www.oqo.es
www.picturebookillustration.blogspot.co.uk
www.picturingbooks.com
www.sarmedemostra.it
www.scbwi.org
www.sevenstories.org.uk
www.societyillustrators.org
www.teatrio.it
www.thelightbox.org.uk
www.theweeweb.co.uk
www.topipittori.it
www.ucalgary.ca/~dkbrown
www.unaflordepapel.blogspot.com
www.zazienews.blogspot.com
www.zoolibri.com

Index

Acknowledgements & Picture Credits

I am greatly indebted to Laurence King Publishing once again for all the support and encouragement received. In particular, special thanks go to Donald Dinwiddie and Ida Riveros who have both played a major role in the putting together of this book. And I wish also to thank Zoe Bather for the design of the book and Simon Walsh for overseeing its printing. Thanks also go to all of the artists and/or their publishers and estates who have generously allowed their works to be reproduced in these pages. And finally, to Sara Fanelli for creating a wonderful cover.

All photography by Ida Riveros, with the exception of the images on pages 16–21, 26–27, 36–37 and 52–55.

Numerals in bold indicate page numbers

14-15 © ADAGP, Paris and DACS, London 2014; **16-17** Images courtesy of Harvard University Library; **18-19** Images courtesy of Ville de Paris, Médiathèque Françoise Sagan, Fonds patrimonial Heure Joyeuse; **20-21** Images courtesy of Harvard University Library; **22-23** © 1926 the Estate of William Nicholson; **24-25** © 1984 Bonaventura & c. © 1986 Adelphi Edizioni S.p.A. Milano; **26-27** Images courtesy of the Special Collections Research Center, University of Chicago Library; **28-29** © 1934, 1962 Ludwig Bemelmans. Used by permission of Viking Penguin, a division of Penguin Group (USA) LLC; **30-31** © Edward Ardizzone Estate 1936, Oxford University Press. Permission granted by the Artist's Estate and Oxford University Press; **32-33** © Edward Ardizzone Estate 1937, Oxford University Press. Permission granted by the Artist's Estate and Oxford University Press; **34-35** Text © Walter de la Mare. Illustrations © Harold Jones Estate 1937, Faber and Faber. Permission granted by the Artist's Estate; **36-37** Reproduced by permission of Country Life, Photographed by Martin Salisbury at The Fry Art Gallery, Saffron Walden; **38-39** © Estate of Edward Ardizzone. Reproduced by permission of the Artist's Estate; **40-41** © ADAGP, Paris and DACS, London 2014; **42-43** © 1941, 1969 Robert McCloskey. Used by permission of Viking Penguin, a division of Penguin Group (USA) LLC; **44-45** Reproduced with permission of Penguin Books Ltd; **46–47** Text © František Hrubin -heirs c/o DILIA, 1943. Illustrations © Jiří Trnka -heirs c/o DILIA, 1943; **48-49** Reproduced by kind permission of the Tom Gentleman Estate; **50-51** © 1945 Enid Marx; **52-53** Images courtesy of Maurizio Corraini s.r.l., © Bruno Munari. Maurizio Corraini s.r.l. All rights reserved; **54-55** Images courtesy of Maurizio Corraini s.r.l., © Bruno Munari. Maurizio Corraini s.r.l. All rights reserved; **60-61** Reproduced by kind permission of Chloe Cheese;

62-63 Reproduced by permission of Country Life; **64-65** © 1952 Tove Jansson © Moomin Characters™; **66-67** © 1953 Graham Greene and Dorothy Craigie; **68-69** © 1953 Joseph Low; **70-71** Illustrations reproduced by kind permission of the Weisgard family; **72-73** © Antonio Frasconi/DACS, London/VAGA, NY 2014; **74-75** © 1956 H.A. Rey; **76-77** © Librairie Hachette, 1956, pages 4-5, 12-13, 20-21; **78-79** First Chronicle Books LLC edition published in 2009 © 1956 by Ann Rand Ozbekhan and Paul Rand. Used with Permission from Chronicle Books LLC, San Francisco. Visit www.ChronicleBooks.com; **80-81** © 1956 Jan Le Witt; **82-83** © Estate of Ben Shahn/DACS, London/VAGA, New York 2014. Text © 1958 Alastair Reid; **84-85** © 1958 André François; **86-87** © 1959 Helen Borten; **88-89** Text © 1959 May Udry. Illustrations © 1959 Maurice Sendak; **90-91** © 1959 Roger Duvoisin; **92-93** © 1959, 1978, 1999 Leo Lionni. Italian edition © 1999 Babalibri, Milan; **94-95** © 1959 H.R. Sauerlander & Co., Aarau, Switzerland. Engligh translation © 1959 Oxford University Press. Reproduced by permission of Oxford University Press and Fischer Verlag; **96-97** © Ladybird Books Ltd, 1959; **100-101** © 1960 Elizabeth Rose; **102-103** © Miroslav Sasek Endowment Fund; **104-105** © 1961 M. T. Grendi; **106-107** © 1961 Michael Foreman; **108-109** Reproduced by kind permission of The Estate of Edward Bawden; **110-111** Reproduction by kind permission of Elfriede Binder; **112-113** Artwork © John Burningham. Reproduced by arrangement with Random House Children's Publishers UK, a division of The Random House Group Limited; **114-115** Reproduced by kind permission of The Edward Gorey Charitable Trust; **116-117** Illustrations copyright © 1966 Brian Wildsmith. Reproduced by permission of Star Bright Books, Inc. and Oxford University Press; **118-119** © 2009 Phaidon Press Limited. Original edition © 1966 Diogenes Verlag AG Zürich; **120-121** © 1967 David Gentleman. Reproduced by kind permission of the artist; **122-123** © 1967 Artemis Verlags-AG, Zurich; **126-127** © 1969 Ezra Jack Keats; **128-129** © John Lawrence; **130-131** Illustrations © 1972 Chihiro Iwasaki. English text © 1972 The Bodley Head; **132-133** Original story and illustrations © 1973 Nord-Sud Verlag AG, Zürich; **134-135** Reproduced by permission of Oxford University Press and Charles Keeping; **136-137** © 1974 William Stobbs; **138-139** © 1976 Seizo Tashima; **140-141**

Text & illustrations by Shinta Cho © Fumi Suzuki 1976; **142-143** © 1980 Shigeo Nishimura; **144-145** © 1981 Maurice Sendak; **146-147** Text © 1981 Ted Hughes. Illustrations © 1981 Leonard Baskin; **148-149** © William Steig, 1982, reproduced by permission of Penguin Books Ltd; **150-151** © 1982 Roy Gerrard; **152-153** © 1984 Alice and Martin Provensen. Reprinted by permission of SLL/Sterling Lord Literistic, Inc.; **154-155** © 1988 Warwick Hutton. Reproduced by kind permission of Lizzie Hutton; **156-157** ©1993 Lisbeth Zwerger, rights arranged with minedition rights & licensing ag Zurich/Switzerland; **158-159** English language edition © Tate 2012. First published in German as Alphabet © Květa Pacovská 1992/2012, minedition; **160-161** © 1996 Éditions MILAN; **162-163** © 1999 Sara Fanelli; **164-165** © Beatrice Alemagna; **166-167** Original edition published by Gakken Education Publishing Co.,Ltd. © 2005 Komako Sakai French edition © 2006 l' école des loisirs, Paris›; **168-169** © Hinstorff Verlag GmbH, Rostock 2007; **170-171** Published in Great Britain in 2008 by Bloomsbury Publishing © 2008 Albin Michel Jeunesse; **172-173** Courtesy of Cai Gao and Hsin-Yi Publications, Taiwan; **176-177** © 2010 Uitgeverij De Eenhoorn bvba; **178-179** © 2010 Topipittori; **180-181** © CASTERMAN S.A; **182-183** © Yanni Kim; **184-185** © CASTERMAN S.A; **186-187** © 2010 Chiaki Okada & Kou Okada; **188-189** © 2010 Nobrow Ltd. All artwork and characters within are © 2010 Bjorn Rune Lie and Nobrow Ltd; **190-191** © Éditions du Seuil, 2011; **192-193** Illustrations © 2011 Jon Klassen. Reproduced by permission of Walker Books Ltd; **194-195** © 2011 Planeta Tangerina; **196-197** Original title: "Tomten är vaken"© Text: Astrid Lindgren, 1960. Saltkråkan AB© Illustrations: Kitty Crowther, 2012. First published by Rabén & Sjögren, Sweden, in 2012; **198-199** Text and illustrations © Marta Altés 2012; **200-201** Illustrations © 2012 Alexis Deacon. Reproduced by permission of Walker Books Ltd; **202-203** © 2012 Sunmi Park; **204-205** © 2013 Cappelen Damm; **206-207** Illustrations © 2013 Laura Carlin. Reproduced by permission of Walker Books Ltd; **208-209** Text and illustrations © 2014 Katherina Manolessou